TO

_____

FROM

_____

_____

_____

_____

THE   LION

BIBLE

To Keep For Ever

Text by Lois Rock
Illustrations copyright © 2013 Sophie Allsopp
This edition copyright © 2013 Lion Hudson

The right of Sophie Allsopp to be identified as the illustrator of this work has been asserted
by her in accordance with the Copyright, Designs and Patents Act 1988.

Published by Lion Children's Books
an imprint of
Lion Hudson plc
Wilkinson House, Jordan Hill Road,
Oxford OX2 8DR, England
www.lionhudson.com/lionchildrens

ISBN 978 0 7459 6914 5
ISBN 978 0 7459 6497 3 (pink)

First edition 2013

Acknowledgments

The Bible references given refer to the major stories of each chapter.

Scriptures quotations are taken or adapted from the Good News Bible © 1994 published by
the Bible Societies/HarperCollins Publishers Ltd UK, Good News Bible © American Bible
Society 1966, 1971, 1976, 1992. Used with permission.

A catalogue record for this book is available
from the British Library

Printed and bound in Estonia, November 2013, LH35

THE LION
BIBLE
TO KEEP FOR EVER

RETOLD BY LOIS ROCK
ILLUSTRATED BY SOPHIE ALLSOPP

LION
CHILDREN'S

Contents

A Promised Land 84

Disaster and Rescue 134

THE NEW TESTAMENT

✳

The Time of Jesus 184

The First Christians 270

God and God's People

Why is the world the way it is? How best should people live in it?

The stories in the first part of the Bible take on these huge questions. The very first story is about God the creator. The world is the way it is because God made it like that – a good and lovely home for every living thing.

The next story is about the first people, Adam and Eve. They chose to ignore God's warnings and questioned their carefree life in a paradise garden. As a result of their rebellion, they found themselves in a harsh world where good and evil were entwined. They felt cut off from the God who had made them.

From that point, the pattern was set: those who lived good lives could also trust that God would take care of them; those who were wicked would suffer the consequences of their wrongdoing.

Yet, long ago, God made a plan to heal the rift between earth and heaven. God chose a man he named Abraham to be the father of a great nation. They would have their own land in Canaan and they would prosper. Through that nation, Israel, God would show the world how to live in the way that was good and right, as friends of God.

Neither Abraham nor his descendants were perfect: far from it. Even so, God did not forget them. When the Egyptians made them their slaves, God sent Moses to lead them back to freedom and to Canaan.

On the way, God gave Moses laws that would guide the people to live as God's friends should. God made an agreement – a covenant. If the people obeyed the laws, God would be their God; they would be God's people. The terms of this agreement were written on tablets of stone and kept in a golden box: the ark of the covenant.

This hymn in the Bible book called Psalms recalls the covenant:

Don't be worried on account of the wicked;
don't be jealous of those who do wrong.
They will soon disappear like grass that dries up;
they will die like plants that wither.
Trust in the Lord and do good;
live in the land and be safe.
Seek your happiness in the Lord,
and he will give you your heart's desire.

Psalm 37:1–4

11

THE STORY OF CREATION

GENESIS 1–2

✳

THE BIBLE BEGINS WITH THE STORY OF CREATION.
IT IS TOLD AS A POEM.

*In the
beginning…
the earth was
formless
and desolate.*

GENESIS 1:1–2

*D*arkness, darkness, deep and wild.
  *Then God began to speak. God smiled
and said, "In my creation I want… LIGHT."
The dark exploded into bright.
The evening dimmed, night passed away,
and morning came: the world's first day.*

*The next day came: God made the sky
— a blue horizon wide and high.*

*The third day: God spoke to the sea
and to the ocean, wild and free:
"Your waves may crash and surge and roar…
but may not go beyond the shore.
For I am making all the land
from ooze and mud, from rock and sand."*

Then God spoke to the humble earth:
"From deep within you, life will birth."
So seeds grew plump, their shoots uncurled,
and tendrils, leaves, and flowers unfurled.
The petals fell, the fruit grew round
and tumbled gently to the ground
among the grasses, ripe with grain,
from which new plants would grow again.

The fourth day: sunshine, warm and gold,
and then the moonlight, silver, cold...
and stars that danced across the night,
each one a tiny twinkling light.

The fifth day: larks on whirring wing
rose from the earth, began to sing;
and then on every field and hill
the birds began to chirp and trill.
Across the dawnlight's dappled sky
they swooped and dipped and soared so high.
While in the oceans, green and dim,
great shoals of fish began to swim
among the corals, wracks, and weeds
and tentacled anemones.

The sixth day came: God spoke again.
"Let creatures run on hill and plain:
the swift gazelle, the lumbering ox,
the sleepy sloth, the wily fox.
The lion, roaring from afar,
the stealthy, silent jaguar.
The fragile lamb… the grizzly bear:
let there be creatures everywhere.

"And last, I now make humankind," said God.
"Their strength and soul and heart and mind
will make them guardians of all:
the wild, the tame, the great, the small.

"For them, the fruit trees will bend low
and grain will in abundance grow
and they will gather from the land
wild harvests grown by my own hand.

"Their children soon will fill the earth
with love and laughter, joy and mirth."

And so God's work at last was done.
The sixth day ended as the sun
sank slowly in the golden west.

The seventh day was time to rest.

God looked at everything he had made, and he was very pleased.

GENESIS 1:31

THE GARDEN OF EDEN

GENESIS 2–3

✳

THE SECOND STORY IN THE BIBLE IS ABOUT ADAM AND EVE AND
HOW THEY LET EVIL INTO GOD'S GOOD WORLD.

G od made the first man from the dust of the
earth. Then God planted a garden to be the
man's paradise home.

There were trees in that garden – beautiful trees
– and a silver stream that watered them and made
their fruit grow plump and luscious.

"I want you to tend this garden," God told the
man. "You may eat any of the fruit that grows
here... except for one sort. In the middle of the
garden is a tree that gives knowledge of good and
evil. If you touch its fruit, you will die."

God watched as the man explored the garden.
First, he ate some fruit. Then he swam in the
stream. Then he lay on the bank and sighed as,
idly, he picked flowers and tossed them aside.

"It is not good for him to be alone," said God.
"I will make a companion for him."

So God took more earth, mixed it into clay, and
fashioned all kinds of animals and birds.

"Look at these," said God to the man. "You are
the one who will give these creatures their names.
From among them you will surely find those that
you can befriend."

*God placed
the man in
the Garden of
Eden to
cultivate it
and guard it.*

GENESIS 2:15

18

So the man gave the animals their names. But though the monkeys chattered at him and the birds sang cheerful songs, the man still had no one to talk to. And though the dog looked up at him with trusting eyes and even the wild cat purred contentedly by his side, the man still longed for someone who would be a true companion.

Then God made a new plan. God caused the man to fall into a deep sleep, and, while he was sleeping, took a rib from his body, closed the wound, and made a woman.

The man smiled to see her. "Here is someone of my own kind," he said. And the man and the woman took delight in being together, unashamed of their nakedness. ↩

Now, of all the creatures God had made, the snake was the most cunning.

It slithered up to the woman as she sat alone in the dappled shade.

"Are you allowed to eat any fruit you like?" asked the snake.

"Oh yes," replied the woman. "There is so much, and it is all delicious. Only the fruit of the tree in the middle of the garden is forbidden, and that is because it would poison us."

The snake flickered its tongue. "Nonsense," it said, and its whole body quivered with mirth. "God just wants to hide a big secret from you.

"If you eat the fruit, you will know not only about good things – which you do already – but evil things too. Then you will be as wise as God."

The woman looked at the fruit. It looked soft and ripe and… yes, it was just within reach.

"I would like to be wise," she said.

So she took the fruit and bit into it. It was delicious. "Come, taste this wonderful fruit," she called to the man.

He came and he too ate the forbidden fruit.

Almost at once, they realized their mistake. They were seeing the world differently. Most of all, they were shocked and embarrassed at their nakedness. At once, they began stitching leaves to make clothes so they could cover themselves. ✍

That evening, God came walking in the garden. The man and the woman were ashamed of what they had done, and they hid.

"Where are you?" called God, and God's voice was that of a friend.

The man stepped out from the shadows. "I... was hiding," he said, "because I was naked."

God frowned. "Who told you that?" God asked. "Did you eat the fruit I told you not to touch?"

The man shook his head. "You can't blame me," he said. "That woman you made to be my friend – she ate the fruit and then she gave some to me."

Then the woman stepped forward, her eyes brimming with tears. "It was the snake," said the woman. "The snake tricked me."

For a moment there was silence. "There will be consequences," said God, and the sound of God's voice seemed to herald the coming of the dark. "From now on, the snake will crawl on its belly, and it will be despised by humankind for ever."

Then God spoke to the woman. "Now your childbearing, which was meant to be so natural, will be painful and difficult."

To the man God said, "From now you are condemned to work for everything. You will toil to make the earth grow crops. The work will wear you out. When your weary life ends, your body will return to the dust from which it was made."

Finally, God sent the man and the woman – Adam and Eve – out of Eden.

They wept as they left their paradise home. They knew they would never again eat from the tree of life. Though their descendants would inhabit the earth, would any of them live as friends of God? ✳

At the east side of the garden God put winged creatures and a flaming sword which turned in all directions.

GENESIS 3:24

THE STORY OF NOAH

GENESIS 6–9

AS HUMANKIND SPREAD ALL OVER THE WORLD, EVIL INCREASED.

God had made a good world, but people had chosen wickedness. Indeed, it seemed that there was always a war going on somewhere, and the fighting was brutal and cruel.

"I'm heartily sorry I made the world at all," exclaimed God. But then he remembered: there was Noah, a man of peace.

God went and spoke to Noah. "I am going to send a flood that will wash this wicked old world away," said God. "I want you to build a boat – an ark – on which to save all that will be needed for a new world to begin.

"You will take your family on it – your wife, your three sons, and their wives. You will take at least one breeding pair of every kind of animal. You will take seven breeding pairs of some of the domestic animals and all of the birds."

Noah listened to God's instructions for how to build the ark: a huge vessel with three decks and a door in the side. He and his sons toiled to make it durable and waterproof. His wife and daughters-in-law gathered supplies by the cartload and loaded them on the boat.

Then it was time to gather the animals. Did the creatures know that disaster loomed? Somehow they came, from their secret places in the hills and forests and marshes, and from the furthest plains: some prancing, some prowling, some plodding. The birds swooped down in tiny flocks and settled on the roof of the ark, while butterflies danced in and out of the entrance until it was time to close the door.

Then, as God had warned, it began to rain. It was as if floodgates in the sky had opened, as water came sluicing down and filled the streams and the rivers until they burst their banks. It made ponds in the meadows and cascades in the mountains. Slowly, steadily, the water began to rise.

The water rose over the houses and the trees. It rose over the hills and covered the mountains.

In all the world there was nothing but Noah and his ark… and still it kept on raining, day after day after day. The weeks turned into months, and the flood covered the earth like a mighty sea. ❧

But God had not forgotten Noah. When the
time was right, God sent a wind that blew the
rain clouds away, and the flood began to go down.
One day, the ark that had drifted for so long
shuddered and shook as it crunched on a ridge
of solid ground. No land was visible, but within
a few weeks Noah and his family saw the tops of
mountains appearing around them like tiny rocky
islands.

"Perhaps there is land beyond what we can see,"
announced Noah one day. "I am going to let a
raven out to see if it can find anything."

The raven flapped into the sky. It flew in
ever-widening circles around the ark until it
disappeared beyond the horizon.

With a little sigh of disappointment, Noah went
to find a dove. "Now you come back," he
said sternly, making the
dove look startled; but
Noah was smiling as he
let the bird go.

The dove fluttered like
silver in the sunlit sky,
then returned to Noah
in a clatter of wingbeats.
"Another time," said Noah.
A week later, Noah sent
the dove out again.
This time, it flew

out of sight and was gone for some
hours. At evening time, however, it
returned with a fresh green olive
leaf in its beak.

Noah almost danced through the ark
as he told the news. "Look at this leaf!
Somewhere the world has been dry for so long
that the plants are growing. The new beginning
has begun!"

When Noah let the dove fly out a week later,
it did not come back. But the mood was one of
excitement. The ground on which the ark was
resting was nearly dry. Then God gave Noah the
instruction he had been longing for:

"It is time to leave the ark. Let the creatures go
free, so they can have young and fill the earth.

"Start a new home for your family: may you have
grandchildren and great-grandchildren.

"And remember this: I promise never again to
destroy living things. The pattern of seasons will
continue for as long as the world exists."

Noah opened the great door. What a joyful noise
there was as the creatures hurried and scurried and
leaped and flew to find new homes. Birds soared
up in the sky before dipping over the horizon. ❧

*"As long as the
world exists,
there will be a
time for planting
and a time for
harvest."*

GENESIS 8:22

A rainbow spread across the sky. "Look," said
God to Noah. "That is the sign of my promise,
my everlasting covenant with all living things." ✳

THE TOWER OF BABEL

GENESIS 11

✳

THIS ANCIENT STORY WARNS HUMANKIND NOT TO GROW PROUD.
IT EVOKES A REAL TOWER THAT WAS BUILT IN BABYLON.

*At first, the
people of the
whole world
had only one
language and
used the same
words.*

GENESIS 11:1

When the world was new, the people all
spoke the same language. If ever there was
something to be decided, they could talk things
over and come to an agreement.

There came a time when they all wanted the same
thing: they had found a good place to settle.

"We've had enough of the wandering lifestyle,"
they said. "It's hard being nomads. No sooner have
we found good pasture than our flocks graze it
bare and it's time to move on again.

"But here on the plains we could make permanent
homes and enjoy a much more comfortable life.

"The land is watered by rivers that flow even
during the dry season. Their flooding has made
the land fertile. We will be able to grow good crops
and prosper."

And so the people became farmers. The land
grew such abundant crops that they had time and
money to think of more than scraping a living.

There was time for making new discoveries and
telling their friends about them.

"Look: can you see how the mud by the river

turns rock-hard as it dries? There's a really practical way to use it: if we mould the mud into just the right shape when it is wet, we can let it dry to make building blocks – bricks.

"If we bake the dried bricks, they get so hard that even the rain doesn't damage them. It's like being able to make thousands and thousands of perfectly cut stones that we can use to build whatever we like.

"And do you know what else we've found? Pits of tar: that black, sticky, gluey stuff. There's loads of it around. It's perfect for holding the bricks together."

As the people talked and listened to one another, they became cleverer and cleverer at making bricks and building walls and decorating them with bright mosaics. ✍

Then they came up with an amazing plan.

"Let's build a city with a tower that reaches to the sky.

"It will be the most amazing structure the world has ever seen.

"We will be famous! We will be powerful! Nothing will be able to stand in our way, whatever we want to do."

Soon the building began: hundreds and thousands of people all working together. There were teams to make the bricks, teams to move the bricks, and teams to lift the bricks up to the teams of skilled workers who laid the bricks according to the agreed design.

There were teams to collect the tar, teams to transport the tar, and teams to make sure the bricklayers had just the right amount ready to hand.

There were teams of craftworkers who planned the mosaics and who told the workers just how to place each piece correctly.

To make the tower resemble a mountain reaching to the heavens, there were teams of gardeners who planned the groves of trees that were to be planted on each platform.

And because the workers all spoke the same language, progress was spectacular. ✎

Then God came down to see the city and the tower.

God looked at the buildings and simply said, "Well, well, well! These people certainly do think highly of themselves. They really believe they can use the mud of the earth to build their way right up to heaven.

"And this is just the beginning of their plans, I can tell. They'll stop at nothing.

"But they can only do so because they speak one language. It's time to mix things up."

And that is what happened. Each team began to use its own special words. If you didn't speak the language, you couldn't be part of the group.

It wasn't long before there were rival teams. The rivalry led to jeering. The jeering was clearly disrespectful, even for those who didn't know what the insults meant.

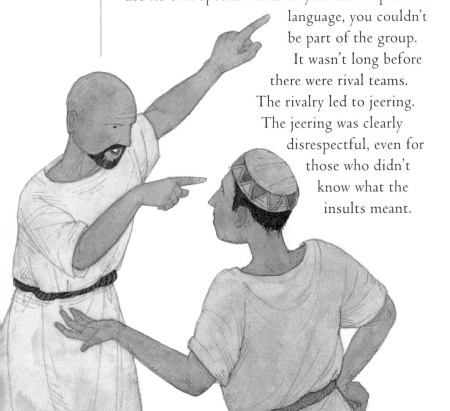

Then the jeering led to scuffling, and scuffling led to fighting, and one by one, the different groups of people just gave up on the building project and went to find a quiet life somewhere else.

They went to the far corners of the earth. Never again would they be able to work together.

And the tower that was supposed to reach up to heaven… well, it never got there. Little by little, it crumbled right back down to earth. ✳

THE STORY OF ABRAHAM

GENESIS 11–13, 15–18, 21

✳

THE BIBLE RECOUNTS THE STORIES OF ONE NATION: THE PEOPLE
OF ISRAEL. THIS IS HOW ISRAEL BEGAN.

Long ago lived a family descended from Noah himself. They lived in the elegant city of Ur, in Babylonia. When the three sons had grown up and married, the father took the entire household further west, to the city of Haran. There they prospered.

Then God spoke to one of the sons: Abram.

"Go," said God. "Leave this settled life. I am going to lead you to a land where you can make a new home. You will have a family, and your children's children will have many descendants. They will become a nation, and through them I will bless the world."

Abram trusted God. He set out with his wife Sarai, his nephew Lot, and all his wealth: flocks of sheep and goats and cattle, and many slaves to help look after them.

They journeyed south to the land of Canaan. Now they were nomads, always moving from place to place in search of new pasture for their flocks and pitching their tents wherever they found good grazing.

*God said
to Abram,
"Through you
I will bless all
the nations."*

GENESIS 12:3

It was a hard life, but even so they grew wealthy. Indeed, the flocks increased so much that Abram and Lot agreed to go their separate ways.

God spoke again to Abram. "Look around you – north, south, east, and west. I am going to give all this land to you and your descendants. They will be so numerous that no one will be able to count them. It will be theirs for ever."

Abram sighed. He had already put his trust in God… but still he and Sarai had no children. Time went by, and Abram remained troubled that he had no heir.

One night, under the dark sky, he complained to God. "Such a wonderful promise you make… and for what? If I have no son, one of my slaves will inherit all my wealth!" ❧

Then he heard God speaking again: "Look at
the sky and try to count the stars; you will have
as many descendants as that." ❧

Abram was reassured, but Sarai remained in despair.

"I'll never have children," she told her husband. "I'm too old. Why not follow the usual custom and sleep with my slave woman? Perhaps she can have a child for me."

Abram did as Sarai suggested, and the slave woman Hagar gave birth to a son, Ishmael. But perhaps it was no surprise that Sarai was eaten up with jealousy. She began to wish that neither mother nor son existed.

God spoke to Abram again. "Be sure of this: I keep my promises. Today I am giving you a new name: Abraham, father of many nations. And your wife will be Sarah – princess. She will be the mother of nations.

"Hagar and Ishmael will have to make their living elsewhere. Ishmael too will prosper and have many descendants. But my promise to you will come true through Sarah's son.

It was some time later that three travellers passed by. Abraham saw them from the shelter of his tent when the sun was high. He welcomed them to stay a while and enjoy a meal.

As they sat eating, the travellers enquired about his wife. "She's in the tent," said Abraham, matter-of-factly.

"Nine months from now," said one of the travellers, "she will have a son."

Sarah was closer than they thought. She was at the door of the tent, listening. When she heard the prediction, she laughed aloud.

"Why is she laughing?" the stranger asked. "Is anything too hard for God?"

To Sarah's own astonishment, she soon discovered she was pregnant. When the child was born, Abraham named him Isaac — a name that means "laughter".

"God has brought me joy and laughter," said Sarah. "Everyone who hears of this birth will laugh with me." ✳

"God has brought me joy and laughter."

Genesis 21:6

41

JACOB AND ESAU

GENESIS 25, 27–33

✳

WHEN ISAAC GREW UP, ABRAHAM ARRANGED FOR HIM TO MARRY
A GIRL CHOSEN FROM AMONG HIS OWN RELATIVES.
HER NAME WAS REBECCA.

Isaac knew of his father Abraham's hopes that his
family would become a nation. He could not have
been more delighted when his lovely wife, Rebecca,
gave birth to twins.

From the beginning, the brothers were very
different. The elder, Esau, had an abundance of red
hair. He grew up loving the outdoor life and became
a skilful hunter. His aging father was delighted to
have so many animals brought home for the pot.

The younger, Jacob, was dark and smooth-
skinned. He preferred to spend his days around the
encampment, where his mother doted on him.

One day, when Jacob was cooking, Esau came
home from hunting utterly famished.

"Mmm," he said, as he came near the cooking pot.
"I need some of that bean soup, Jacob."

The younger brother looked up slyly. "It'll cost
you," he said.

"Whatever you want," said Esau, uncaring.
"I'll die if I don't get some food."

"Good," replied Jacob. "Then you

won't mind giving me all the rights due to the firstborn son."

Esau hardly heard him. "Yes, of course," he said. "What's the use of rights? You can't eat them."

There was a pause. "Do you really promise?" Jacob demanded.

"Yes, I do," snapped Esau. "I promise my little brother that he can have my big-brother rights. Now where's that soup?"

Esau got his meal and was satisfied; but Jacob was serious about the matter… and so was Rebecca. Mother and son watched and waited as Isaac grew old and blind. Rebecca overheard when a frail Isaac called Esau to him.

"Go and hunt for something tasty," he said. "Cook me a delicious meal, and I'll give you the final blessing which is due an elder son."

Rebecca rushed to find Jacob. "We must make our move now," she whispered.

Together they agreed to make a tender, aromatic stew from ordinary goat meat. Jacob would wrap himself in the goatskins so he would smell and feel like Esau… and then go and claim the blessing.

The ruse worked. When Esau returned and took his stew to his dying father, he discovered the ugly truth: Isaac had prayed for Jacob to be the son who would gain both wealth and power.

"I'll kill the traitor," Esau raged. ❧

Isaac prayed this for Jacob: "May those who curse you be cursed, and may those who bless you be blessed."
GENESIS 27:29

*God made this
promise to Jacob:
"Remember, I
will be with you
and protect
you wherever
you go."*

GENESIS 28:15

Rebecca knew Esau was in an ugly mood and likely to carry out his threat. "You'll have get away from here," she warned Jacob. "I'll tell your father that it will be best for you to find a wife from among my relatives. None of us are happy that Esau is so fond of Canaanite girls, so he's bound to agree."

So it was that Jacob soon found himself making the lonely journey north. The first night he slept under the stars with only a stone for a pillow. But in a dream he saw a stairway reaching from earth to heaven, with angels going up and down. He heard God speaking to him: "I am the God of Abraham and Isaac. I will give this land to you and your descendants. They will prosper, and they will bring my blessing to the world."

The next day, Jacob journeyed on. In time he reached the home of Rebecca's brother – his uncle, Laban.

He received a warm welcome. "You'll have to work, of course," said Laban. "But you can't work for nothing just because you're a relative. How much pay do you want?"

Jacob had already decided – because he had fallen in love with Laban's younger daughter.

"I'd like to marry Rachel," he said. "I will work for seven years without pay."

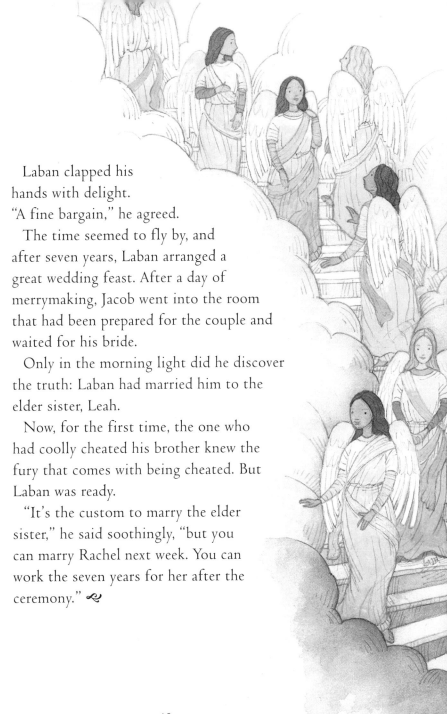

Laban clapped his
hands with delight.
"A fine bargain," he agreed.

The time seemed to fly by, and
after seven years, Laban arranged a
great wedding feast. After a day of
merrymaking, Jacob went into the room
that had been prepared for the couple and
waited for his bride.

Only in the morning light did he discover
the truth: Laban had married him to the
elder sister, Leah.

Now, for the first time, the one who
had coolly cheated his brother knew the
fury that comes with being cheated. But
Laban was ready.

"It's the custom to marry the elder
sister," he said soothingly, "but you
can marry Rachel next week. You can
work the seven years for her after the
ceremony." ❧

Jacob had no choice but to agree. He worked diligently and the flocks increased, but he and Laban could not be friends. After years of bitterness, they agreed to part. Jacob gathered up his wives, his servants, his children, and his share of the flocks, and set off for Canaan.

"This is the only way open to me," he said to himself. "Yet it sends me closer to my brother. I am leaving one enemy only to have to face another."

Jacob prayed to God to help him. He chose the finest animals from his flocks to give to Esau as gifts, but he remained anxious about the inevitable meeting. In the night, a stranger came and fought with him. For all they grappled, neither could win. "I won't let you go," hissed Jacob, "unless you say a prayer of blessing for me."

The answer was puzzling: "You will no longer be Jacob," said the stranger. "Your name will be Israel: the one who struggles with God."

And then Jacob knew: he had seen God face to face.

The very next day, Jacob saw Esau coming with an army of fighting men. Jacob rushed to bow down in front of him.

"What's going on?" laughed Esau. "Why have you sent servants trying to foist your gifts on me?

"We're brothers, Jacob. And our quarrel is over." ✳

JOSEPH AND HIS DREAMS

GENESIS 37, 39

✳

GOD HAD GIVEN JACOB A NEW NAME: ISRAEL.
HIS DESCENDANTS BECAME KNOWN AS THE PEOPLE OF ISRAEL,
THE ISRAELITES.

Joseph was Jacob's favourite son.

Jacob was the father of twelve fine sons; but he was particularly fond of the two who had been born to his beloved wife, Rachel. The younger was Benjamin, and Joseph was the elder.

When Joseph was a young man, Jacob gave him a beautifully patterned coat. It was not just a costly garment; it was a status symbol – a clear sign that Jacob intended Joseph to receive all the privileges that should be due the eldest son.

Joseph knew it, and he let it be known how much he looked down on his half-brothers.

"I had a dream," he told them one day, "about us harvesting the wheat. We were all tying sheaves, and then my sheaf stood up. Yours gathered around in a circle and bowed down."

The brothers guffawed mockingly.

"Dream on," they sneered. "We'll never bow down to you."

48

Not long after, Joseph had another dream. Undaunted, he told it to his family. "You'll never guess," he said, "but in my dream the sun, the moon, and eleven stars bowed down to me."

That annoyed even Jacob. "You can be too arrogant," he scolded. "Don't go imagining that I, your mother, and all your brothers will ever bow down to you."

Even so, Jacob continued to treat Joseph differently from the other brothers. He sent the ten eldest off to look after the flocks in a distant pasture while Joseph stayed at home. When the ten had been gone some time, he sent Joseph merely to find out if all was well.

The brothers saw him coming and began to grumble and scoff about him. The talk took an ugly turn.

"I could murder that brat. I'll rip that coat off his shoulders if he begins to swank around in it."

"I wish some lion would take a fancy to it. To him, in fact."

"We could... you know... pretend that a lion attacked him. Shove his body down a dry well. Mess up the coat a bit. Who's to know?"

"Just a moment," said the eldest, Reuben. "We can throw him down a dry well and give him a scare. But lay off the violence. That's just wrong." ❧

Joseph brought bad reports to his father about what his brothers were doing.

Genesis 37:2

49

As Joseph reached his brothers, they were ready to pounce on him. They laughed as they threw him into a well and they laughed as they left him, begging for mercy from the shadowy depths.

Then, in the distance, they saw traders passing on the dusty road bound for Egypt.

"We can sell Joseph as a slave," whispered the brother named Judah. "Then we'll be rid of him, and our consciences will be clear." ✍

Reuben had not been part of Judah's plan to sell Joseph. He was distraught when he found out what his brothers had done. "What am I going to say to our father?" he raged.

Together they agreed to deceive Jacob. They took Joseph's coat, ripped it up, and dipped it in the blood of one of their own goats. They went home and showed the limp rag to Jacob, telling him that it was all they had found of Joseph. And Jacob wept.

Even so, in faraway Egypt, God took care of Joseph.

He was sold as a slave, but at least it was to an honest man who also happened to be a senior officer of the palace guard. This man, Potiphar, recognized Joseph as intelligent and hard-working. He quickly promoted him, putting him in charge of the running of the household.

God was with Joseph and made him successful in everything he did.

GENESIS 39:3

Then Potiphar's wife began to take an interest in Joseph. "It's a pleasure to have you here," she told him. She pressed closer and added, giggling, "Does anyone ever tell you how handsome you are?"

Joseph realized at once that she was being overly friendly.

"I've gained my master's trust," he said firmly. "I'm not going to betray it for anything."

But Potiphar's wife would not leave him alone. One day, when no other servants were near, she grabbed him by the clothes. He struggled free, but the woman clung on to his outer garment.

Then she began to scream. "Look! That slave tried to get into bed with me! He tried... he tried ... oh, it's too awful!"

When Potiphar came home, his wife showed him Joseph's clothing and easily convinced him that Joseph had behaved abominably toward her.

"I'll have him arrested!" shouted Potiphar. "He'll go to jail and rot there."

The future looked bleak. ✴

JOSEPH AND THE FAMINE

GENESIS 39–46

✳

THE PRISONER JOSEPH THOUGHT HIS DREAMS WERE OVER.
BUT EVENTS TOOK AN UNEXPECTED TURN, AND ALL BECAUSE
OF THE KING — THE PHARAOH.

G od can take care of the worst situations. At
least, that was what Joseph came to believe as
he tried to rebuild his life in an Egyptian prison.

He played his part – trying to forget the
injustice that had been done to him and behaving
faultlessly. It was not long before the jailer put him
in charge of the day-to-day running of the place.

Some time later, two of the pharaoh's servants
arrived in the same prison. One night, they both
had dreams that troubled them. Joseph offered to
explain the meaning.

Pharaoh's butler spoke first. "I dreamed of a
vine, with blossom and then grapes and newly
squeezed wine," he said.

"You will be set free and once again serve wine at
the royal table," said Joseph. "When that happens,
please tell the pharaoh about me and help me get
out of prison. I never did anything wrong."

Pharaoh's baker was encouraged. "I dreamed of a
basket of pastries," he said. "Then birds swooped
down to peck them."

*Joseph said,
"It is God who
gives the ability
to interpret
dreams."*

GENESIS 40:8

Joseph drooped his head in sorrow. "I am sad to say your dream means bad news. You will be executed and birds will eat your corpse."

Both predictions came true. But though the butler was pardoned and went back to his job in the palace, he forgot about Joseph... until the pharaoh had puzzling dreams that none of his advisors could explain. Then the butler remembered.

"There is a young foreigner in the royal prison who can explain dreams," he said. "He foretold my being pardoned."

At once, servants were dispatched to bring Joseph, and the pharaoh described his dreams.

"In one," he told Joseph, "I was standing on the banks of the River Nile. Seven fat cows came up out of the water. As they ate the green grass, seven thin ones came and ate them.

"In the other, I saw seven ears of grain. They stood plump and ripe in the golden summer sun. Then seven more stalks grew, thin and dry. They simply swallowed up the fat ears of grain."

Joseph nodded sagely. "The two dreams mean the same thing," he said. "Seven years of abundant harvest will be followed by seven years of famine. You need to choose someone to organize the storage of grain from the good years to last through the bad." ✌

At once, the pharaoh chose Joseph. He made him governor of Egypt and gave him the second royal chariot to ride in. Wherever he rode in it, a guard of honour went ahead, ordering people to make way.

Through the seven years of good harvests, Joseph made sure that surplus grain was carefully stored. Then came the famine. Joseph was in charge of the distribution of food: first to the Egyptians, and then to foreigners who came to buy – for the famine was everywhere.

Among those who were suffering from hunger were Joseph's old family, back in Canaan. They had heard there was food in Egypt, and one day, Jacob sent Joseph's ten half-brothers to buy some. They were nervous even of the slaves who ushered them to see the governor. They bowed low when they were in his presence.

All at once, Joseph remembered the dreams he had had as a young man. His brothers were bowing down. Even though they had not recognized their brother, the prediction had been correct.

But Joseph could not forget how they had treated him. He questioned them sharply, desperately trying to find out about his one true brother without revealing who he was.

"To prove you're not spies," he snapped, "one of you must stay as a hostage. Then bring that younger brother you claim to have, to prove that you're telling me the truth about yourselves." ✑

Joseph said, "God has made me forget all my sufferings."

GENESIS 41:51

Jacob was dismayed when the brothers returned
and told him of the Egyptian's demands. "My dear
wife Rachel only had two sons," he wept. "I've lost
Joseph. I can't bear to let go of Benjamin."

But the famine grew more severe, and soon there
was no choice. The brothers returned to Egypt,
taking Benjamin with them.

When Joseph saw his one true brother, he made
a plan. He gave the brothers a feast while his
servants loaded up sacks of grain. He told his
head servant to slip his precious silver goblet into
Benjamin's sack. The next day, he sent the brothers
on their way. Then he sent a servant after them.

"Stop!" cried the man. "One of you is a thief. My master's silver goblet is missing."

The brothers denied that they had done any wrong, but one by one the sacks were searched. There, in Benjamin's sack, was the goblet.

"My master has said he wants the culprit as a slave," snarled the servant. "The rest of you can go."

The brothers were distraught. They knew how they had wronged their father in getting rid of Joseph. Now they were desperate to take Benjamin safely home. They insisted on going back to see if they could change the governor's mind.

Judah was still tormented by guilt about his part in selling Joseph. He stepped forward in front of the official who had power of life and death over him. "Take me as a slave in place of Benjamin," he said.

Then Joseph knew: his brothers were truly sorry for what they had done to him. He could not pretend any longer.

"Look!" he cried. "I'm Joseph! Is my father still alive? Don't worry about what you did long ago. It was all part of God's plan to keep our family safe through this famine. Now hurry and fetch my father. You must all come and live in Egypt."

And so Joseph's entire family became one. ✳

Joseph said to his brothers, "God sent me ahead of you to rescue you in this amazing way."

GENESIS 45:7

SLAVES IN EGYPT

Exodus 1–2

THE FAMILIES OF JACOB AND JOSEPH PROSPERED IN EGYPT.
THE LAND THEY WERE ALLOTTED GREW CROPS IN ABUNDANCE.

Hundreds of years passed. A new pharaoh became ruler of the land – one who knew nothing about Joseph and the events of the famine long ago. What concerned him was the number of Israelites living in Egyptian territory.

"Foreigners," he warned his advisors. "We can't count on their loyalty. They might even join with our enemies to defeat us. We must keep them under strict control."

First, he made them his slaves. He ordered his slave-drivers to make them work unbearably hard. "That way they won't have the spirit or the energy to make trouble," he laughed. "My building projects need thousands upon thousands of bricks. Forcing the Israelites to toil in the mud to make them is a perfect solution."

But the Israelites were strong. Though they lived in poverty, healthy babies continued to be born. The pharaoh ordered the midwives who helped deliver the Israelite babies to make sure all the newborn boys died. But the two midwives believed in God: bravely, they ignored his order.

The midwives feared God and so did not obey the pharaoh.

EXODUS 1:17

Then the pharaoh issued a new order: every Israelite baby boy must be thrown in the river. He sent his soldiers to enact his cruel plan.

There was one Israelite mother who refused to be defeated. When she had a baby boy, she kept him well hidden. But after three months, she knew she needed a cleverer plan.

"Look," she said to her daughter Miriam. "I've made a basket and covered it with tar. That has made it watertight, so it will float. We're going to cradle your brother inside and put him in the river ourselves."

The mother left her baby among the reeds and sedges. Miriam hid a little way off to see what would happen next. ❧

There came the noise of laughing and chattering.
A princess of Egypt was coming with her maids to
bathe in the river.

As she stepped down into the water, the princess
saw the basket. Curious, she asked a maid to fetch
it for her.

She lifted the lid and saw…

"A baby!" ❧

Amid much giggling, the princess picked up the baby, and then all the maids pleaded to be given a turn at cuddling him so he wouldn't cry.

"I think I know why he's here," said the princess. "This is an Israelite baby boy, and someone is trying to keep him safe. Well, I think I shall make him mine so I can keep him safe for always."

When Miriam heard this, she almost gasped aloud. Her mind was racing. What if she never saw her brother again? And then she had an idea so brilliant that she burst out of her hiding place before she had time to worry about what might happen.

The princess named the boy "Moses".

EXODUS 2:10

"Do you need a nurse for that baby?" she said. "Someone who's just lost a baby of her own and could feed him and look after him?"

The princess turned to look at the girl – with the dark hair of an Israelite and the grime of living in poverty. She smiled knowingly.

"Yes please," she said.

Miriam went and brought her mother.

"Will you look after this lost little baby for me?" the princess asked the woman. "I'll pay you."

The baby's mother agreed at once. She raised her own son in safety until he was old enough for the princess to adopt him and raise him as a prince. ✳

Moses hears God's call

✳

MOSES GREW UP IN LUXURY AS AN ADOPTED PRINCE.
YET HE KNEW HE WAS AN ISRAELITE.

When Moses was a young man, he went to visit the brickfields. There he saw the slaves toiling in the mud under the relentless sun.

"So these are my people," he mused. "This is how they live."

He was shocked to see how thin they were, how they bent under their heavy loads, and how the slave-drivers beat and whipped them.

From behind, he heard shouting. He turned and saw an Israelite picking himself up off the ground and clenching his fists menacingly. The Egyptian slave-driver struck him again. He kicked the fallen man until he was quiet.

"He's killed him," whispered Moses.

Then his anger boiled over. He ran over and hurled himself at the slave-driver, punching and kicking till the man could fight no more. Moses smiled as the man slumped. But his satisfaction vanished when the man collapsed and died.

"No!" Moses whispered to himself. "I could get into so much trouble for what I've done... something I didn't really mean to do." He looked around in a panic. Perhaps he could cover the whole thing up. Panting heavily, he dragged the body to a shallow ditch, and shovelled sand over it to hide it.

The next day, in spite of his misgivings, he went back to the same place. To his dismay, he saw two Israelites fighting.

"Why are you hurting each other?" he demanded to know. "Can't you settle a quarrel better than that?"

"What right do you have to criticize?" sneered one, pushing his face close. "Who put you in charge around here anyway? Are you going to kill me like you killed the Egyptian yesterday?"

Moses went cold with fear. His crime had been seen. Fearful of the consequences if the news got out, he fled the country. ✦

God saw the slavery of the Israelites and was concerned for them.

EXODUS 2:25

Out in the wild lands beyond Egypt, he found a welcome with a shepherd named Jethro. In time, he married one of Jethro's daughters and took care of his father-in-law's flocks.

One day, he led the sheep and goats across the stony desert to a high mountain called Sinai. As he sat, he saw something puzzling. From a distance, it looked like a bush that was bright with flames... and yet it wasn't being burned up.

"I think I'll take a closer look at that," he said to himself.

As he walked nearer, he heard a voice: "Moses! Moses!"

Moses looked around. He could see no one. "Here I am," he answered hesitantly.

"Do not come closer," said the voice. "Take off your sandals, for this is holy ground. I am the God of your ancestors, the God of Abraham, Isaac, and Jacob."

"I have seen how my people are being mistreated. I am choosing you to lead the Israelites out of Egypt and to freedom."

Moses was overawed by what he was hearing. "But what will I do if they won't listen to me?" he asked. "Why should they believe that it is you who have sent me?" ✌

Moses asked God for his name. God replied, "I am who I am."

EXODUS 3:14

68

"See the stick you have in your hand?" replied God. "Throw it to the ground."

Moses did, and at once, it became a wriggling snake. Moses shrank back in fear.

"Pick it up by the tail," said God. Moses did, and it became a stick again.

God showed Moses other wonders he could work to convince the Israelites that he was really sent by God. Still Moses protested.

"I don't speak well," he said. "You know that I fall over my words."

Did God sigh… or was it just the wind? After a long silence, God spoke again.

"Your brother Aaron is a good speaker," said God. "I will tell you what you must do, and he can be the spokesperson."

So Moses went back to Jethro and told him of all that had happened. Jethro agreed to let him go with his wife and children. Then, as God had foretold, Aaron came to find him. Together they went to Egypt and gathered the Israelites. They told them of God's plan to set them free. They showed the wonders that God had given them power to work.

The people were convinced and said prayers of thanks to God for coming to their aid. ✻

"Please, God," said Moses, *"send someone else to set the Israelites free."*

Exodus 4:13

MOSES AND THE PHARAOH

EXODUS 5–12, 14

✳

THE STORY OF MOSES AND THE ESCAPE FROM EGYPT IS TOLD IN
THE SECOND BOOK OF THE BIBLE, EXODUS. THE WORD ITSELF
MEANS "COMING OUT".

M oses and Aaron went to the pharaoh.
"We bring a message from the God of our
people," they said. "Let the Israelites go, so they
can hold a festival of worship in the desert beyond
Egypt's borders."

The pharaoh almost laughed aloud. "God?" he
said. "Do the people Israel have a God? I've never
heard of such a being, and I won't let the people
go.

"In fact, I think you're just trying to get them a
few days off work. They're my slaves, and they stay
here."

After Moses and Aaron had gone, the pharaoh
spoke to his slave-drivers.

"I fear rebellion. Keep those Israelites busy. Up
until now you have provided them with the straw
they mix with the mud to make bricks. Let them
go and fetch their own straw – but demand the
same number of bricks. Then they won't have time
to pay attention to those two troublemakers."

When the people found out they were to be

punished with extra work, they complained bitterly to Moses. Moses in turn complained to God.

"I will make the pharaoh listen," said God. "The people of Egypt will soon discover that I am God."

As God commanded, Moses and Aaron returned to the pharaoh to renew their request.

"Watch what God can do," declared Aaron. He threw down his stick and it turned into a snake.

The pharaoh snapped his fingers to summon the court magicians. They came and threw their sticks to the ground, and the sticks became a writhing mass of snakes.

At once, Aaron's snake swallowed all the others.

The pharaoh glared. "I don't change my mind just because you can do an entertaining trick," he said. "My slaves stay here."

Moses and Aaron were sent away. They felt dispirited that their brave attempts had failed. But God gave them new courage. "The king goes down to the River Nile each morning," said God. "Meet him there in the morning. I will work a new wonder there." ◆

God said to Moses, "Tell the Israelites this: I will rescue you and set you free from slavery."

Exodus 6:6

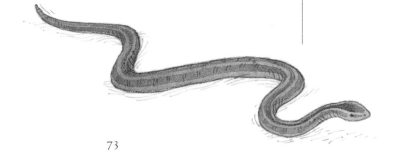

73

God said to
Moses, "Tell the
Israelites this:
I will bring
you to the land
that I solemnly
promised to give
to Abraham,
Isaac, and
Jacob."

EXODUS 6:8

Moses and Aaron went to the river. When the
pharaoh arrived, they struck the water with Aaron's
stick, and it turned to blood. All over the land, in
water channels and pools and pitchers, the water
turned to blood and became undrinkable.

The pharaoh was contemptuous. He simply gave
orders for new water channels to be dug, and made
a point of turning away from Moses and Aaron.

The two pursued him with a solemn warning.
"If you do not show respect for our God, disasters
will befall all Egypt," they said.

First, there was a plague of frogs that came
hopping out of the Nile and invaded everywhere,
jumping into beds and baking pans.

Then there were swarms of gnats, swirling in
the air and droning mercilessly. Next came flies,
buzzing from dungheap to dining
table. Disease devastated the
Egyptians' flocks and herds.

Moses went to the king and
ceremoniously threw handfuls
of ashes before him. "Disaster
will spread like dust," he said.
Not long after, all the

people and the animals were covered with boils and open sores.

After that, hail rained down on the crops and ruined the harvest. Great clouds of locusts arrived, blown in on the desert winds. Then thick dust darkened the sky for three terrifying days.

Though the pharaoh sometimes wavered, he never gave way to Moses' demands.

"The next disaster will put an end to your stubbornness," Moses told him. "Throughout the land, the firstborn in every Egyptian household will die."

Moses also went to warn the Israelites. "On the day I tell you, every household must prepare a final meal to eat in Egypt. Kill a sheep or a goat to cook and eat, and mark your doors with some of the blood. Make bread quickly, without yeast. Be dressed for a journey, with sandals on your feet.

"Death will strike the firstborn all over the land, but death will pass over the houses that are marked as I said. In the face of so much death, the pharaoh will plead with us to leave his land." ✍

Moses said, "When your children ask you, 'What does this ritual mean?' you will answer, 'It is the sacrifice of Passover to honour God, because he passed over the houses of the Israelites in Egypt.'"
EXODUS 12:26–27

The tragedy that engulfed the nation made the pharaoh give in. He allowed Moses to lead the Israelites out of Egypt.

Then, in a final panic, the pharaoh sent his charioteers to bring his slaves back. God made a pathway through the sea for the Israelites. While behind them the waters closed over their enemies, God's own people walked to freedom. ✳

THE ARK OF THE COVENANT

EXODUS 16–40

✳

ON THE JOURNEY FROM EGYPT TO CANAAN, GOD MADE A
COVENANT, OR AGREEMENT, WITH THE ISRAELITES. GOD WOULD
BE THEIR GOD IF THEY WOULD LIVE AS GOD'S PEOPLE.

Between Egypt and the land of Canaan lay a
bleak and dusty wilderness from which tall and
mysterious mountains rose.

Very soon, the Israelites' rejoicing at their escape
gave way to murmuring and complaining.

"What's the use of freedom if we have nothing
to live on?" they said. "Back in Egypt we had those
lovely little vegetable plots. It was sometimes hard
watering them – but there was water, wasn't there?
Enough to grow cucumbers and melons, as well as
lovely fat leeks, plump garlic, and enormous onions.

"And remember the places we could go fishing.
There was food for free. Not like here.

"We could die out here."

Yet Moses trusted God to guide them
and keep them safe. Surely it was a
miracle that made water gush from
a rock when Moses struck it with
his stick? Could it be any power
except God's that made flocks
of quails land around the camp

78

so the people could catch them for the pot? Who but God could send the dew that turned to sweet, crackly flakes of manna for the people to collect each morning?

"We must obey the God who takes care of us," Moses told the people.

He led them to the foot of Mount Sinai – the very place where he had seen the burning bush and heard the voice of God. He now understood that he was the person who would help the people hear that voice and the call to holiness.

Moses went up the mountain alone. There, God gave him the terms of the covenant – the agreement – that the people must honour. At the heart of it were ten great commandments:

One: Worship no god but me.

Two: Neither make any idols nor bow down to any.

Three: Do not claim you are acting in God's name when in fact you are doing wrong.

Four: Observe one day in seven, the sabbath, as a day of rest.

Five: Respect your mother and your father.

Six: Do not murder.

Seven: Do not be unfaithful in marriage.

Eight: Do not steal.

Nine: Do not accuse someone who is innocent.

Ten: Do not allow yourself to long for what belongs to another. ❧

God told Moses to say these words to the people of Israel: "If you will obey me and keep my covenant, you will be my own people."

Exodus 19:3, 5

Moses stayed at the top of the mountain for some time. Far below, the people began to complain to Aaron. "Maybe Moses will never come back. You must provide us with another god we can worship."

Aaron was anxious to please them. He told the people to collect gold jewellery from their wives and children. He melted the metal and poured the liquid into a mould. In this way, he made a golden calf.

"This is the god who led us out of Egypt," declared Aaron. "Tomorrow there will be a festival of worship, and then we will have a feast."

The festival turned into a riotous party. On the mountaintop, God told Moses to hurry down with the laws, which had been engraved on two tablets of stone. As he reached the camp, Moses heard the singing and saw the dancing, and he knew that the people had forgotten what was right and what was wrong. Furious, he smashed the tablets of stone. Then he overturned the golden calf, melted it, and ground the gold to a powder which he mixed with water.

"Drink this!" he ordered the people. "There will be no more gold for any idol while I am leader."

The ringleaders were severely punished, and the rest of the people repented of their wrongdoing. Moses went a second time to the top of the mountain to rewrite the laws on new tablets of stone. ✌

Moses went back to God and prayed this prayer: "Please forgive the people their sin."

EXODUS 32:32

After that, he turned his attention to teaching
people the Law — the ten great commandments and
more besides: laws about how to worship God and
what festivals to celebrate; laws about how to treat
one another fairly; laws about showing kindness
and justice to outsiders.

He passed on the instructions God had given
him for making a place of worship. As the people
were themselves nomads, it was to be a tent — a
tabernacle. He asked the people to bring their
gifts of wood and metal, leather and cloth for its
construction. Those who were skilled were set to
work: some making the posts and the frame, others
the coverings; yet others the curtain to divide the
tabernacle into two rooms.

There were furnishings to be made too, including
a gold-covered altar on which to burn incense,
another on which to lay offerings, and a golden

lamp stand with seven branches on which lamps were to be kept burning. Moses chose the people who were to serve as priests, and elaborate garments were made for them to wear.

A craftworker with the finest skills was asked to make a gold box in which to keep the tablets of the law that were the terms of the people's agreement with God. This became known as the "ark of the covenant".

When at last everything was ready, the ark was brought into the innermost room of the tabernacle, and all the furnishings put in their appointed places. The priests led a ceremony of worship.

Then a cloud covered the tabernacle, and a dazzling light shone from within it. It was the light of God's own presence with his people. ✳

"Never forget these commands that I am giving you today."

DEUTERONOMY 6:6

A Promised Land

The people of Israel firmly believed that from ancient times, God had promised them a land – a good place in which they could make their home. They believed this was the land of Canaan.

They had not settled the land this way in the time of Abraham, Isaac, and Jacob. Instead, they had herded flocks and lived as nomads there.

They had built permanent homes during their years in Egypt and had grown crops there, but they knew that Egypt could never be their home.

Then Moses had started them on the journey back to Canaan. He appointed Joshua to be the nation's leader after him and to claim the land. It was Joshua who divided the land between all the great families of the nation.

There were times when all seemed well. More and more, however, the nations that lived in and around Canaan challenged the new settlers. They came raiding, plundering, harassing. In these violent times, the people were proud of their own warrior heroes – Gideon, Samson, and others like them. However, unless the people agreed to keep God's laws and live as God's people, the disasters were bound to keep on happening.

The story of Ruth, set in these times, is a more hopeful tale: a tale of loyalty rewarded, of traditions honoured, of God's blessing.

After years of turmoil, a godly leader emerged: Samuel was a source of wisdom and justice. When he grew old, the people wanted to be sure of strong leadership, and they demanded a king.

The first, Saul, seemed brave and honest, but he lacked confidence in himself, in Samuel, and in God. David, by contrast, was inspired. Even in the face of great danger, he seemed to be able to trust God.

The words of this psalm are believed to be those of David, who began life as a shepherd boy:

The Lord is my shepherd;
I have everything I need.
He lets me rest in fields of green grass
and leads me to quiet pools of fresh water.
He gives me new strength.
He guides me in the right paths, as he has promised.

PSALM 23:1–3

David was respected as a fighter and loved as a leader. He brought the nation through troubled times to victory and peace. He did not always remember to obey God's laws, but he was deeply sorry for wrongdoing and equally enthusiastic in his worship.

His son, Solomon, basked in his father's success. His reign seemed to be a golden age for Israel. The Temple he built in Jerusalem became a symbol of the people's devotion to God and the place where the ark of the covenant was kept safe.

Joshua and the Land of Canaan

Joshua 1–3, 6, 8–22, 24

✳

THE ISRAELITES SPENT MANY YEARS AS NOMADS IN THE
WILDERNESS BETWEEN EGYPT AND CANAAN. MOSES GREW OLD
AND CHOSE JOSHUA TO BE HIS SUCCESSOR.

*God said to
Joshua, "Be
determined,
be confident;
and make sure
that you obey
the whole Law
that my servant
Moses gave
you."*

JOSHUA 1:7

Joshua was a leader that everyone could admire. Not only was he a brave and skilful warrior; he also respected God's laws and let God direct all he did.

"Get ready," he told the people. "We are about to begin the long campaign to settle the land of Canaan – the land God promised to our people long ago."

He began by sending two spies into Canaan, and they secretly made their way to the walled city of Jericho. They slipped among the shadows, listening to what the townsfolk were saying about the threatened attack. All too soon, the sun was setting and the guards at the city gate were getting ready to lock up.

A woman named Rahab agreed to shelter them for the night. She hid them under the bundles of flax that were drying on the flat roof of her home. That night, when the king's men came asking what she knew about two foreigners, she lied.

"They were here," she agreed, "but they left before sunset."

While the soldiers set off on a useless quest to hunt down the men, Rahab hurried to fetch the spies.

"Come quickly," she said. "My house is built into the city walls. I know how I could lower you to the ground outside through a window."

Before they made their escape, the spies gave Rahab a promise: "Tie this red cord to the window, and when we attack, we will spare you and all your family."

The spies returned to the Israelite camp. "We are bound to win," they told everyone. "The people are terrified."

Joshua ordered the priests to take the ark of covenant and lead the way across the River Jordan and into Canaan. By a miracle, a sudden landslide blocked the flow of water so the people could cross on dry land.

When they all reached Jericho, God told Joshua what to do.

"Arrange a procession like this: first an advance guard, then seven priests blowing trumpets. Behind them, other priests are to carry the ark of the covenant aloft. The rest of your fighting force are to follow behind. ࡀ

Rahab said, "I know that your God is God in heaven above and here on earth."

JOSHUA 2:11

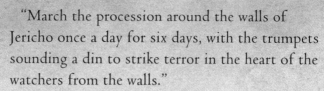

"March the procession around the walls of
Jericho once a day for six days, with the trumpets
sounding a din to strike terror in the heart of the
watchers from the walls."

Joshua obeyed.

On the seventh day, the instructions were
different. This time, the whole procession marched
round the walls in silence. Seven times they
marched. Joshua gave a sign. The trumpets gave a
long, wailing blast. The people shouted out their
war cry.

The walls of Jericho crumbled. The Israelites
captured the city. ❧

Rahab and her family were led to safety. From that day forward, they were accepted by the people of Israel.

That first great victory was followed by many others. Joshua became greatly feared by the kings of the many city states of Canaan. He was skilled in the tactics of war and ruthless in wiping out his enemies.

When the Israelites had taken possession of the land, God gave them peace.

JOSHUA
21:43–44

Above all, Joshua was convinced that God was with him. He firmly believed that Canaan was theirs because of God's choosing. When all the battles had been won, Joshua decided where each of the tribes of Israel would settle.

He gathered the leaders of the people together. "This land is ours because of what God has done for us," he declared. "Make sure that you obey the law that Moses gave us: serve God with all your heart and with all your soul."

Years passed. The people of Israel prospered in the land. Its soil was rich and fertile, and rains came in their season. They were able to feast on grapes from vines that the Canaanites had planted; they gathered olives from ancient groves.

Joshua watched the progress of his people with mixed feelings. As he grew old, he feared for what might happen when he died. Once again, he called the people together.

"I hear news that troubles me," he said. "I hear that some of you are tempted to worship foreign gods: gods of Egypt, gods of our long-ago ancestors – even the gods formerly worshipped in this land of Canaan.

"This is not part of our covenant with God. If you fail to obey God's laws, then God will not protect you. The nation will be destroyed. I and all my household are resolved to worship God and God alone. Now tell me your choice."

Then the people all said this: "We will serve the Lord our God. We will obey his commands." ✳

Joshua said, "As for me and my household, we will serve the Lord."

JOSHUA 24:15

GIDEON ASKS FOR A SIGN

JUDGES 2, 6–8

✳

THE PEOPLE OF ISRAEL BELIEVED THAT GOD HAD HELPED THEM
MAKE CANAAN THEIR HOME. EVEN SO, THEY WERE AFRAID THAT
ONLY THE CANAANITE GODS HAD POWER IN THE LAND.

The Israelites were eager to believe that living
in Canaan was a promise fulfilled. But who
controlled the weather? What god decided if the
harvest would be plentiful? The nations who had
for long years dwelled in Canaan believed it was
their own gods. Surely, thought the Israelites,
it would do no harm to keep the local
traditions of worship.

They were mistaken. When they were
disloyal to their own God, enemy
nations came raiding and plundering.
Among the fiercest were the Midianites.
They came with their livestock and tents and
camped on land that the Israelites
had claimed as their own. They
destroyed the crops and took
sheep and cattle and donkeys.
Wherever the Midianites came,
the Israelites had to flee to
caves among the hills.

It was for this reason that, one

day, a young farmer named Gideon chose to thresh his harvest grain in secret – inside a low-walled wine press. A stranger came and sat under a tree nearby.

"God is with you," said the stranger, "and you are a brave and mighty man."

Gideon glared at him. "I don't know why you think God is with any of us," he said curtly. "God may have brought us out of Egypt, but now we're at the mercy of the Midianites."

"You should rescue your people," said the stranger.

He spoke with an authority that unsettled Gideon. "Prove to me that your message is from God," he demanded.

"Very well," said the stranger. "Prepare a meal of meat and bread and put it on that rock there."

Gideon obeyed. The stranger touched the food with his stick – and at once, it burst into flames and crumbled to ash.

The miracle convinced Gideon of God's calling, but he was afraid to act openly. Under cover of night, he went and tore down the altar that had been built by his own father to honour the most powerful of the foreign gods. When the people of the town found out, they were horrified.

His father spoke up for him: "If the gods care about the way the altar has been treated, then they can punish Gideon." ✎

Gideon said, "I have seen God's angel face to face!"

JUDGES 6:22

The angry mob waited and watched. Nothing happened. Emboldened, Gideon blew on a trumpet to summon any who dared come and fight alongside him.

"Let us drive out our enemies!" he cried.

Many answered the call… then, once again, nervousness overcame Gideon.

"O God," he prayed, "give me a sign that I am doing the right thing. I shall put a fleece out on the ground overnight. In the morning, may I find dew on the wool but not on the ground."

The prayer was answered. Gideon squeezed a bowlful of water from the fleece. Yet he remained troubled.

"Just one more sign," he pleaded in his prayers. "This time, may the ground be wet with dew and the fleece dry."

When Gideon saw the sign, he set out with thirty-two thousand fighting men to face the Midianites.

"You have too many men," said God. "I want the people to see that it is I who will

bring victory. Tell anyone who is scared that they can go home."

Twenty-two thousand men hurried back to their farms and their families.

"Ten thousand is still too many," said God. "Take the men down to the stream to drink. Those who kneel down to get at the water can go. Keep only those who stay alert, scooping the water up to their mouths."

That test left Gideon with just three hundred. They found the Midianites and their allies encamped in a valley – as many as in a swarm of locusts.

Gideon went ahead with just one servant to spy on them. He overheard two soldiers talking.

"You won't like this," said one, "but I had an awful dream. In it, a loaf of bread came and squashed a tent flat. What do you make of that?"

"I think that's a dreadful sign," came the gloomy reply. "I take that as a warning that this rebel Gideon is going to beat us." ❧

Gideon told his men, "God is giving you victory over the Midianite army!"

JUDGES 7:15

Greatly encouraged, Gideon returned to his tiny army. He divided the men into three groups of a hundred each. "We will make our move tonight," he told them. "I am giving each of you a trumpet, a blazing torch, and a jar to hide the flame.

"I will go with one group," he told them. "The other two must position themselves so that we surround the camp between us. When I give the sign, let everyone smash their jar, hold their torch high in their left hand, and blow their trumpet."

Silently, secretly, they all got ready. In the fearful dark, Gideon gave the sign. Suddenly, shockingly, torchlight blazed around the enemy camp. Three hundred trumpets blared out. Their eerie wailing was followed by a chilling war cry: "A sword for God and for Gideon."

Panic swept through the Midianite camp: the fighting men began to attack one another in the dark and, terrified, they all began to flee.

Gideon and his men pursued them boldly and inflicted a crushing defeat. ✳

Gideon told the people, "I will not be your ruler, nor will my son. God will be your ruler."

JUDGES 8:23

SAMSON AND THE PHILISTINES

✳

To the south of the land of Israel lived a warrior people. Many years had passed since these Philistines had first invaded from lands across the sea.

The Philistines had won for themselves only a narrow strip of land by the coast. Inland dwelled the Israelites; but the Philistines scorned them. Ruthlessly, they set out to plunder their wealth, and God allowed this to go on for forty years.

There lived in Israel a man named Manoah, whose wife had never been able to have children. One day, a stranger came and told her that she would have a son.

"You must dedicate him to God," explained the stranger. "You must never cut his hair: it will be the sign that he is God's servant. He will begin the work of rescuing Israel."

Manoah was puzzled when his wife told him the news, but the stranger came and reassured him. When the child was born, the couple named him Samson. He was handsome, healthy… and incredibly strong.

He also grew up to be self-willed and arrogant.

"What I want," he told his parents one day, "is

The child Samson grew and God blessed him.

JUDGES 13:24

for you to arrange my wedding. I've fallen in love with a Philistine girl."

Manoah and his wife were very upset, but Samson was used to getting his way. As the three went down to meet her family, they heard a young lion roaring. On impulse, Samson dashed away, caught the lion, and killed it. Then he went on with the journey and completed his wedding plans.

A few days later, Samson was travelling the same road for the wedding and he decided to go and find the carcass. He was astonished to see that bees had made a honeycomb inside.

At the feast, while he was drinking and boasting with thirty young Philistine men, he remembered this unusual sight.

"I've got a riddle for you all," said Samson. "If you can guess its meaning before our week of feasting is over, there'll be a prize of the finest clothing. Here it is:

"Out of the eater, something to eat;
Out of the strong, something sweet."

The young men were baffled. They were also sly. A few days later, they sidled up to Samson's bride and asked her to wring the answer from him. She found out for them, and they went to claim their prize. ✑

Samson was furious. He marched off to another of the Philistine cities. There he killed thirty young men, pulled the clothes off their bodies, and took them to those who had answered the riddle. Then he went back to his own people.

When he calmed down a little, he went to visit his wife.

"Oh, what a surprise to see you," said her father. "I thought you'd left her for ever. I agreed she could marry your best man."

Samson's anger returned, hotter than ever. "I'll have revenge on the lot of you," he shouted.

He went and caught three hundred foxes, tied them together in pairs by their tails, and put a blazing torch in the knots. Then he sent them running through the Philistines' cornfields. So began his bitter campaign: one Israelite fighter against the enemies of his people.

Though Samson was merciless toward the Philistine warriors, he still had an eye for the lovely Philistine girls. The day came when he fell hopelessly in love with Delilah. The Philistine kings, seeing that they were a couple, went to her in secret.

"We want you to trick Samson into telling you what makes him so strong," they said. "We'll reward you with a handsome amount of silver."

Delilah agreed to help them. She asked Samson for the secret of his might, but Samson fobbed her

Samson led Israel for twenty years while the Philistines ruled the land.

JUDGES 15:20

off with one teasing answer after another.

"You're making a fool of me," she sobbed. "You don't really love me."

She wept and she wheedled, and finally Samson gave in.

"Listen," he said. "I was dedicated to God as a child. That's why I have uncut hair. If my hair were to be cut, it would cut my connection to God and to the strength God gives me."

Delilah knew this must be the truth. Eagerly she went to tell the Philistine kings, who made a plan: she would cut Samson's hair while he slept, and a band of armed men would come and make Samson their prisoner. ✍

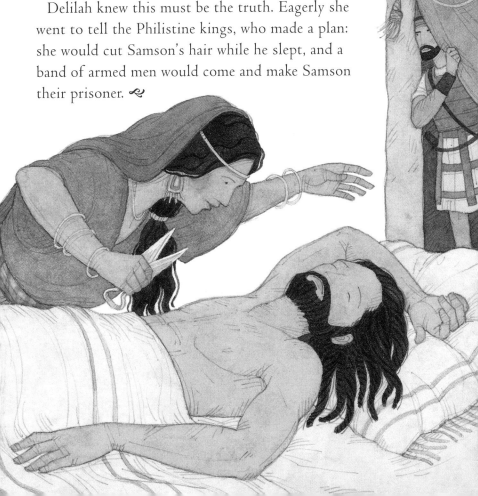

In this way, Samson was betrayed and defeated. The Philistines put out his eyes and threw him into jail. They kept him in chains of bronze and made him do the work of an ox, pushing the huge wooden beam that turned the millstones.

Some time later, the Philistines held a festival.

"Our god has given us victory at last," they cried jubilantly. The celebrations became a riotous party.

"Let's fetch Samson," said someone. Everyone roared with laughter, and a message was sent to the prison.

Samson was brought into the temple, shuffling behind the boy who led him because he could no longer see. For a while, he stood with his head bowed. But already he knew: his hair had grown and his strength was returning.

"Hey, boy," he grumbled to the lad at his side. "Put my hands on the pillars. I'm so weary – I need something to lean on."

The boy did as he was asked. Samson bowed his head and felt his hair swinging around his shoulders.

He said a final prayer: "Please, God, let me get even with the Philistines one last time."

With a great heave, he pushed apart the twin pillars of the temple. The roof crashed in on him and thousands of his people's tormentors. ✻

Samson said this prayer: "God, ruler of all, please remember me. Give me my strength just once more."

JUDGES 16:28

Ruth and Naomi

Ruth 1–4

✳

THE NAME "BETHLEHEM" MEANS "HOUSE OF BREAD". THE
FIELDS AROUND THE TOWN YIELDED ABUNDANT HARVESTS. SO IT
WAS A DISASTER WHEN A SEVERE FAMINE STRUCK.

Elimelech lived in the hilltop town of
Bethlehem. Usually he made a very good living,
but when the harvest failed, he decided to go and
make a new life elsewhere. He went with his wife,
Naomi, and their two sons to the region of Moab.
While they were there, Elimelech died. Naomi's
hope for a happy old age rested with her two
sons, who had married Moabite women.

Then came further tragedies: the
two sons died. Naomi was
unhappy at being alone in a
foreign country. When she
heard that the harvests in
Bethlehem were good once
more, she decided to go back
to her kin.

She set out with her two
daughters-in-law. They had not
gone very far when Naomi
changed her mind.

"It is not right that

you should come with me," she said. "Go back to your mothers. May each of you be able to marry again and have families of your own."

The two young women both started crying. "We want to stay with you," they said.

"No," insisted Naomi. "Your hope of a good future is with your own people."

After more tears, one of the women nodded sadly and set off down the road.

"I still want stay with you," wept the other, whose name was Ruth. "Please don't turn me away."

At last, Naomi relented. The two walked the long miles to Bethlehem.

At their arrival, all the local women began to chatter excitedly. "Is it really you, Naomi?" they asked. "Has life been good to you?"

"Life has been cruel," replied Naomi. "When I left here, I had plenty. Now I have nothing, unless you count bitter memories."

"You have me," Ruth kept on reminding her. She was eager to find ways to help Naomi, and one day, she had a good idea.

"The fields here are ready to be harvested. I'm sure I would be allowed to gather some grain from them. You have told me that gleaning is part of your tradition." ✒

Ruth said to Naomi, "Your people will be my people, and your God will be my God."

Ruth 1:16

Naomi agreed to let Ruth go and, early the next morning, she went to the fields. She walked a little way behind the harvesters, gathering the stalks they had left. She was still gathering when the owner, Boaz, came along. He had to ask his servants who she was, but when he found out, he smiled and went to talk to Ruth.

"You are welcome to go on with your gleaning," he said. "I have heard of your kindness to Naomi." ❧

Naomi was astonished at what Ruth brought home that evening. She had gathered a huge amount of grain – and even had the leftovers from the meal she had been asked to share.

"May God bless Boaz!" exclaimed Naomi. "He is related to me. I think the best plan now is for you to glean only from his fields. You're going to be well looked after there!"

The harvest came to an end, but Naomi could not forget Boaz and his kindness.

She called Ruth to her. "I think it important that you find yourself a husband," she said. "It's quite clear that Boaz wants to take care of you... and the custom is that he should! That's how our tradition says families should look after one another."

She explained to Ruth the right way to go and ask Boaz to marry her.

Ruth felt shy but determined as she put the plan into action.

Boaz was astonished at her request... but he was also delighted.

"May God bless you!" he said. "You are so loyal and kind. However, there is someone else in Bethlehem who is an even closer relative of Naomi's family. I must find out if he will agree to the arrangement."

In the presence of all the town elders, the deal was done. Ruth married Boaz and, in due time, gave birth to a son: Obed.

Naomi's friends came to congratulate her. "You're a grandmother!" they said. "You have a family again, and can look forward to a happy old age."

Naomi loved the little boy as much as if he were her own. "And so the family line will go on," she said, and she smiled. ✳

Ruth's baby boy was Obed. He became the father of Jesse, who was the father of David.

RUTH 4:17

SAMUEL OBEYS GOD

1 SAMUEL 1–7

✳

WHEN THE ISRAELITES MADE CANAAN THEIR HOME, THEY
ERECTED THE TABERNACLE AT A PLACE CALLED SHILOH. THE
SHRINE BECAME A PLACE OF PILGRIMAGE.

Every year, a man named Elkanah used to make
a pilgrimage to Shiloh. He would take his
family with him and give a share of the festival
food to each of his wives and children. That left
the wife named Hannah very sad; it was a bitter
reminder that she had no children.

One year, she left the family party in tears and
went into the shrine itself. Really, she wanted to
scream, but she mouthed her prayer silently. "O
God, let me have a child. Then I will dedicate him
to be your servant."

The aging priest, Eli, watched her indignantly.
"Are you drunk?" he accused her.

Hannah explained why she was so upset, and Eli
relented. "May God answer your prayer," he said.

By the same time the following year, Hannah did
indeed have a baby son whom she named Samuel.

"I will not go to Shiloh this year," she told
Elkanah, "but when the child is old enough, I will
take him there and ask the priest to accept him as
a pupil."

*Eli said to
Hannah, "May
God give you
what you have
asked him for."*

1 SAMUEL 1:17

Hannah was sad to leave her child when that time came. The following year and every year after, she made a new set of clothes for him and took them when she visited at festival time.

Meanwhile, Eli was delighted with his young helper. His grown-up sons were supposed to be the priests after him, but they were utterly disrespectful – both toward their father and toward the religious ceremonies. Samuel, by contrast, was honest and dutiful. ✍

Hannah said this: "God has filled my heart with joy."

I SAMUEL 2:1

When Eli grew old and almost blind, Samuel took on the job of sleeping in the shrine itself, to make sure that the lamps that stood in front of the precious ark of the covenant burned steadily through the darkness.

One night, he heard someone calling his name. At once, he ran to Eli. "Here I am," he said.

"Why are you waking me?" grumbled Eli. "Go back to bed."

Samuel returned to his bed and was just dozing off in the dim light when he heard his name being called. Quickly he ran to Eli.

"You called me, so here I am," he said.

Eli shook his head. "I didn't call and I still don't need anything," he said.

He pulled the blanket over his head to indicate that Samuel should go.

The same thing happened a third time.

Then Eli understood. "Go back to bed," he said. "If you hear the voice again, you will know that God is calling you. Say this: 'Speak, Lord, your servant is listening.'"

There, in front of the ark that contained God's laws for the people of Israel, God told Samuel that Eli's sons were going to be punished for their wrongdoing.

The following morning, Eli was anxious to know what God had said to Samuel. When he heard, he sighed deeply. ❧

Eli said, "God is the Lord; he will do whatever seems best to him."

1 SAMUEL 3:18

"It is only right," he said. "I know I have failed to direct my sons as I should have."

The punishment that Samuel had warned of was not long in coming. The Philistines gathered for war against the people of Israel. In the first major battle, they inflicted a crushing defeat.

The Israelites panicked. "We must make sure God fights with us," they clamoured. "Let's go and get the ark of the covenant and take it with us into battle."

Eli's two sons agreed to the plan and carried the ark between them. Not for a moment did they worry about one very serious matter: they had not been obedient to the laws that were kept within it.

When the Philistines saw that the Israelites had brought with them the most sacred symbol of their God, they were terrified. Fear, however, made them fight more boldly. They won the battle, slaughtered Eli's sons, and carried the ark away as a trophy.

The victory was short-lived. When the Philistines put the ark in their own temple, the statue of their god Dagon fell down in front of it. Then disease swept through Philistine territory and everyone feared that the God of Israel was punishing them. Soon the Philistine leaders agreed to load the ark on an ox cart and send it back to Israel along with gifts of gold.

The Israelites were overjoyed to have the ark

returned and put it into safe keeping. Meanwhile, Eli had died of grief and the people had recognized that Samuel alone was fit to replace him.

"You must turn to God with complete sincerity," Samuel told the people. "Get rid of all the statues and symbols of foreign gods. Worship God alone as the laws require."

Under Samuel's wise leadership, the Israelites succeeded in driving the Philistines back to their own territory. Samuel was respected in all Israel as the one who could help people see right from wrong and live at peace with one another. ✳

Samuel said, "God has helped us all the way."

1 SAMUEL 7:12

Saul: King of Israel

I Samuel 8–11, 13–16

✳

For many years, Samuel led the people of Israel wisely;
but to whom could he hand on the leadership?

Everyone in Israel respected Samuel and trusted
his judgment. As he grew old, he planned
to hand the work of advising people and settling
quarrels on to his sons. The people would not
accept his choice.

"Your sons don't care about justice," they said.
"They only care about who gives them the biggest
bribe.

"We want a king like the other nations that
surround us have. We need someone who will lead
us in war and fight our battles."

Samuel was very unhappy and he prayed to God
for advice. "Give the people fair warning," replied
God. "A king will demand that men fight his wars.
He will make people pay taxes to provide him with
luxuries. The people will regret their choice, but
you have to do as they ask."

Not long after God had said this, two young
men set out on the most ordinary of quests: a
farmer's son and his servant went looking for
some donkeys that had gone missing. After a
fruitless day's searching, the servant suggested

*God said to
Samuel, "You
are not the
one they have
rejected; I am
the one they have
rejected as their
king."*

I Samuel 8:7

they go and visit the holy man who lived in the area.

"He's bound to know where they are," said the servant confidently.

The holy man was Samuel. As the young men approached, God spoke again to the aging leader. "Over there you see the one I have chosen to rule my people."

Samuel invited the men to stay with him that night. "Don't worry about he donkeys," he said. "They've been found."

In the morning he walked with them to the edge of town and then sent the servant on ahead. He took a jar and poured olive oil over the farmer's son's head in the traditional ceremony of choosing.

"God has chosen you to be the nation's king," he said. "Today you will meet a band of holy people. You will get caught up in their lively procession and, as you dance to the music, you will know that God is with you."

Samuel's predictions for the day proved true, and not long after, he summoned all the people to a great gathering. With great ceremony, he first selected the tribe from which he would choose the king. Then he selected the family, but he could not find the one he was looking for. ❧

All the people shouted, "Long live the king!"

I Samuel 10:24

117

God spoke to Samuel. "Look – over there. The future leader is hiding among the baggage."

Samuel ordered Saul to be brought to the front. "Here is the man whom God has chosen," he declared. The shouts and cheers showed that the crowd agreed with Samuel's choice.

Then all the people went home, and Saul to his father's farm. One month passed quietly, but then messengers arrived from another region of Israel.

"An enemy tribe has defeated us in battle," they said. "They are threatening cruel punishments."

Saul was coming in from ploughing when he heard the news. Furious at the wickedness of the people's enemies, he sent messengers to summon an army. His hastily assembled fighting force hurried off on a rescue mission.

It was a triumph and Saul grew bolder. He decided to lead a campaign against the nation's old enemies, the Philistines. That would confirm to himself and everyone that he was fit to be king.

The campaign proved to be a disaster. Saul's men found themselves vastly outnumbered and they were forced back into an untidy retreat. Saul lay low, hoping that Samuel would keep his word and come to perform the proper religious ceremonies before the next battle. But the days went by and he did not arrive.

Saul was desperate. "I shall perform the ceremonies myself," he announced. "We cannot wait for ever."

Saul said to the people, "This is the day God rescued Israel."

I SAMUEL 11:13

He had only just finished when Samuel arrived, his face furrowed with anger.

"You have not obeyed God," Samuel warned the king. "There will be consequences."

Saul felt lost without Samuel's support. He feared the Philistine weapons, for his enemies had mastered the art of working with iron, and their swords and spears held their sharpness; by contrast, the Israelites had only makeshift weapons. Dare he act? Should he wait? Saul wavered.

Then one of Saul's young fighters acted alone: Saul's own son Jonathan led a daring raid that threw the Philistines into confusion. Saul pressed home the victory. It was the first of many and Saul began to feel proud of what he had done.

Some time later, Samuel returned to Saul with fresh instructions: "God wants you to go to war against the people of Amalek. They have been the people's enemies since the days of Moses, when they attacked our people in the wilderness. Now is the time to destroy them and all their wealth."

Saul went bravely into battle and won.

"It doesn't seem right to destroy the flocks and herds we have captured," he told his soldiers. "I say we keep them."

When Samuel found out, he was furious. "Why do you refuse to obey God?" he demanded to know. "This really will be your downfall." ❧

Samuel gave Saul this warning: "You rejected God's command, and God has rejected you as king."

I Samuel 15:26

As Samuel left, God spoke to him just as he had done years before. "It is time to choose a new king," he said. "Go to Bethlehem, to a man named Jesse. One of his sons will be the next king."

Samuel went and saw Jesse's eldest son Eliab, who was tall and handsome. "That's the one!" he thought to himself.

"No, it isn't," he heard God say.

So Samuel asked to see Jesse's other sons: all fine young men. "But God is not telling me to choose any of these," he thought. So he asked Jesse aloud, "Have you no other sons?"

"Only one," said Jesse. "The youngest is out taking care of the sheep."

"Bring him to me," said Samuel.

They brought David: a young man with laughing eyes who could hardly hold back from picking out a tune on his home-made harp.

"That is the one," said God.

At once, Samuel took a jar of olive oil and poured it over David's head: the traditional ceremony of choosing. ✳

God said to Samuel, "People judge by outward appearances, but I look at the heart."

I SAMUEL 16:7

KING DAVID

I SAMUEL 16–19, 21–23, 27–31; 2 SAMUEL 1–5, 9

✳

DAVID KNEW HE HAD BEEN CHOSEN TO BE KING AFTER SAUL.
HE DID NOT MOUNT A CHALLENGE BUT WAITED PATIENTLY FOR
HIS TIME TO COME.

*"David is a
good musician.
He is also
a brave and
handsome man,
a good soldier,
and an able
speaker. God is
with him."*

I SAMUEL 16:18

The nation's first king, Saul, felt abandoned. Samuel would no longer advise him. When he tried to pray, God seemed far away. He became deeply depressed.

"Perhaps it would be helpful to hire a musician," suggested his servants. "Some soothing harp music might cheer you."

Saul agreed. "I can recommend a young man from Bethlehem," said a servant. "One of the sons of Jesse."

The young man was David. Saul liked him and his music, and summoned him whenever he felt despairing.

There were plenty of reasons for Saul to be worried: chief among them was the evidence that the Philistines were once again getting ready for battle. Saul led his men out to meet them, and the two armies camped on opposite hills overlooking a valley.

One morning, a man named Goliath strode out of the Philistine camp. He was extraordinarily tall and strong, towering over his shield bearer. He wore glittering bronze armour and had a bronze javelin slung over his shoulder. His heavy spear had a fearsome iron blade, as did the sword that was tucked into his belt.

"Listen up, you snivelling cowards," he shouted at the Israelites. "Choose your champion – just one brave man who will fight me. A single contest to settle the war!"

Saul's soldiers grimaced at the words. None of them dared volunteer for such an unequal fight. Saul's promise of great rewards did not tempt them to risk their lives. The challenge went unanswered.

It so happened that David's three elder brothers were in the army, and one day, David arrived with food from home. When he heard Goliath, he was indignant.

"I'll take him on," he declared. "I can't see why anyone is afraid of that lumbering bully."

News that a volunteer had been found was relayed to Saul. When he found out it was David, he was dismayed.

"You're only a boy," he warned. "Goliath is an experienced soldier."

David shrugged. "I'm a shepherd," he said. "I can kill bears and lions. I'm sure I can beat that godless brute." ❧

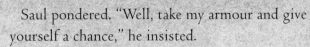

Saul pondered. "Well, take my armour and give yourself a chance," he insisted.

David tried the armour, but it was very heavy. "I'll fight the way I already know," he said.

He walked down to the stream in the valley and chose five smooth stones. Then, sling in one hand and stick in the other, he sauntered toward Goliath.

"Don't mock me," shouted Goliath. "I'm not a dog you can beat with a stick."

"I come to win," cried David. "I am fighting in the name of the great God of Israel." He put a stone in his sling, swung it, and threw.

It was a vicious hit. Goliath stumbled and fell. As David raced forward to kill him with his own sword, the Philistine army began to run – defeated and humiliated.

The whole nation was delighted at David's victory: in song and dance they proclaimed him their hero. Although Saul was grateful to have seen off the enemy, it wasn't long before he began to grow jealous.

"I know you think he should be one of our elite fighters," he grumbled to his son Jonathan. "But I'm suspicious of him."

In fact, Saul more and more often wished the young man dead.

David was forced to flee for his life. He went and lived as an outlaw in the caves among the hills. Over time, other runaways came and joined him. They became a fighting squad in their own right, sometimes hiring out their services to the Philistines, other times taking on Israel's enemies and finally defeating the Amalekites.

After years in the wilderness, the news that David had been expecting and dreading came: both Saul and Jonathan had been killed in battle. It was time to claim the throne.

David waged a clever campaign both to defeat the nation's enemies and to win the support of all the people. When he had done so, he sent soldiers to capture a hilltop fort in the heart of the Israelite territory. He made it the capital city of his united nation and gave it a new name: Jerusalem.

One day, as he was looking back on all his triumphs, David remembered Saul and the happy days he had spent as part of his household.

"Are there any of Saul's relatives left?" he wanted to know.

"There is one," a servant told him. "Saul's grandson, the son of Jonathan. His name is Mephibosheth. He is crippled in both feet."

When Mephibosheth was summoned to court, he was more than a little afraid, but David welcomed him as a friend.

"I am giving to you and your family all the land that belonged to your grandfather Saul," he said. "Its harvests will provide for all their needs.

"As for you, I am inviting you to live at my expense, as part of my household.

"For Saul's family were once good to me, and you deserve my loyalty and kindness." ✳

"I know that God's goodness and love will be with me all my life; and God's house will be my home as long as I live."

LINES FROM PSALM 23, A PSALM OF DAVID

Solomon and the Temple

2 Samuel 5–6; 1 Kings 1–3, 5–8

✳

It was David who chose Jerusalem to be his capital city, but it was his son Solomon who carried out his grandest ambition — to build a temple there.

David and all the Israelites took the ark of the covenant up to Jerusalem with shouts of joy and the sound of trumpets.

2 Samuel 6:15

David, the victorious king, had a fine palace built for him in his capital city, Jerusalem.

He also wanted to honour the God whom he believed had protected him through all the years. He chose the highest patch of ground within the city walls as the place to set up the tent of worship. Then he arranged for the ark of the covenant to be brought there in a jubilant procession.

What he dreamed of was building a proper temple. The tent of worship was a reminder of the Israelites' time of homelessness, when Moses had led them from Egypt to Canaan. Now they were a settled nation, victorious in battle. Surely it was right to honour their God with a building finer than the royal palace?

But David still had battles to fight and quarrels to settle. When he died, the ark of the covenant was still sheltered only in the tent.

The son who became king after him was Solomon. He had been an intelligent child who loved finding out about the world around him. He soon realized the huge task that faced him as king and he went to great lengths to worship God in an elaborate ceremony.

One night, in a dream, God spoke to Solomon.

"What would you like me to give you?" God asked.

"Give me the wisdom I need to rule your people with justice and to know the difference between good and evil," Solomon replied.

"You have asked for the right things," said God. "You will indeed have wisdom, and wealth and honour too." &

One day, two women came to Solomon's court.
"We have a bitter quarrel to resolve," said one.
"We live in the same house and we both had a baby
within two days of each other. Her baby died and
now she has stolen mine."

"You shameless liar," interrupted the other.
"It was your brat who died."

Even as they stood before the king, the two
women began to argue and scream at each other.

Solomon asked a soldier to bring a sword.
"I have decided," he said calmly. "The child will be

cut in two, so each of you can have half."

The soldier grabbed the baby and lifted the glittering blade.

"No, no, no!" wept one of the women. "Let her have the child."

But the other woman said, "Go ahead – cut it in two."

Solomon motioned for the soldier to put down his sword. "Give the baby to the first woman here," said Solomon. "She is clearly the mother, for she loves the child more."

Because of his wise judgments, Solomon earned the respect of his people. Surrounded by peace and prosperity, he saw that the time was right for him to carry out his father's wishes.

"It will be a temple that the whole world will admire," he said.

Solomon ordered the finest materials: for the outer structures, stone, cedar wood, and bronze; for the inside, pine and olive wood, both intricately carved. He needed gold too, in great quantities: gold to cover the floor and the walls, as well the sacred furnishings.

The innermost room was the Holy of Holies: there he placed two gold statues in the shape of fierce and beautiful creatures whose wing tips touched. In the shelter of the wings he placed the ark of the covenant, containing the stone tablets on which the Law was written. ✌

Solomon said, "God promised my father David this: 'Your son, whom I will make king after you, will build a temple for me.'"

1 KINGS 5:5

"May God always be with us; may he never leave us, or abandon us."

I KINGS 8:57

When the ark was in its rightful place, the room was filled with the dazzling light of God's presence.

Solomon stood outside the Temple and prayed aloud, while all the people watched in awe.

"O God," he said, "I have built a majestic Temple in your honour.

"I know that it cannot be large enough, for heaven itself is not large enough to hold you.

"Even so, I ask that, when I turn to face it, you will hear my prayers.

"I ask you to hear the prayers of your people.

"Teach us to do what is right, and bless us."

Then Solomon spoke to the people. "May you always be faithful to the Lord our God, obeying all his laws and commands." ✳

Disaster and Rescue

As a young king, Solomon had been famous for his wisdom. As he grew older, he grew more selfish and made heavy demands on his people: to work on his grand projects; to pay for his luxurious lifestyle; to support his hundreds of wives.

Tellingly, he lost his respect for God. Among his wives were many foreign women, and Solomon built shrines to gods and himself began to worship in them.

When Solomon died, a proportion of the nation rebelled against his son.

The nation split. In the northern kingdom of Israel, one faithless king followed another. In the end, it fell to enemy invaders, and the people were scattered to other lands.

In the southern kingdom of Judah, rulers and people had more respect for God. They survived when Israel did not. They rediscovered God's laws and recognized their importance.

Even so, the king of Babylon came and defeated them. The invaders destroyed Solomon's golden Temple. The ark of the covenant was never seen again.

As the people looked back on their history, they came to believe that this disaster had been because of their faithlessness. Many of the people of Judah – the Jews – were taken away to live in Babylon. They could not have a temple there, but they strove to stay faithful to the Law.

If they did, then surely God would rescue them.
A poet wrote these words:

The thought of my pain, my homelessness is bitter poison;
Yet hope returns when I remember this one thing:

The Lord's unfailing love and mercy still continue,
Fresh as the morning, as sure as the sunrise.
The Lord is all I have, and so I put my hope in him.

LAMENTATIONS 3:19, 21–24

The time came when the Jews did return to Jerusalem
and rebuilt their city and their Temple. They had began
to dream of the time when God might send a new king
– a king like David – who would enable them to live as
God's people again.

THE NORTHERN KINGDOM

I KINGS 9–19, 22; 2 KINGS 1, 9

✳

WHEN KING SOLOMON DIED, HIS KINGDOM WAS SPLIT IN TWO.
IN THE NORTHERN KINGDOM OF ISRAEL, THE KINGS AND THE
PEOPLE FORGOT TO OBEY THEIR GOD.

K ing Solomon's wealth and wisdom made him
famous. However, as the years went by, he
grew careless about keeping God's laws. He also
made heavy demands on his people, so he could
live in luxury. When he died, the people he had
ruled hoped that his son Rehoboam would treat
them more kindly.

They were disappointed: Rehoboam threatened
to be even more severe. There was a revolt, and
the kingdom was split in two. The smaller part
was Judah, where Rehoboam stayed in charge. The
larger was Israel, whose people chose a man named
Jeroboam to be king.

"It is a real problem that our territory does not
include Jerusalem," Jeroboam fretted. "My people
cannot go to worship in the Temple there."

In order to give the people a place to worship,
he arranged for two shrines to be built within his
kingdom. In each of them he placed a golden calf.
In doing so, he broke the covenant: if his people
would not live as God's people, then they could

no longer count on God to protect them.

Israel was ruled by one faithless king after another. Ahab was the worst of all. He married a foreign princess named Jezebel and built a temple to her god Baal in his great city of Samaria.

Jezebel was delighted. "I also want to have my own prophets to lead the worship of my god," she insisted. "And I must get rid of those fools who say they are prophets of the God of Israel."

She gave the order for the prophets she so detested to be hunted down and put to death.

One prophet was steadfast in his loyalty to God. His name was Elijah, and he went to Ahab with a stern message. "God says this: there will be no rain in Israel for two years — or even three. There will be no rain until I say so."

Then he strode far away from the king and queen who wanted him dead. Through the drought and the hardship, Elijah trusted in God to provide for him and was thankful when, by a miracle, ravens brought him food.

After some time, Elijah went back to Israel. Ahab was out looking desperately for any sign of pasture in the long-dry riverbeds. He scowled when he saw Elijah.

"So there you are at last — the worst troublemaker in Israel." ✑

Ahab did more to arouse God's anger than all the kings of Israel before him.

I KINGS 16:33

*Elijah said,
"Answer my
prayer, O
God, so that
the people will
know you are
God, and that
you want them
to return to
worshipping
you."*

I KINGS 18:37

"You're the one making all the trouble," replied Elijah, "because you disobey God.

"I will show you your foolishness. Summon the people to a contest on Mount Carmel. Bring with you Jezebel's prophets who worship Baal and his goddess Asherah."

It was all arranged. On the mountaintop, Elijah ordered the prophets of Baal to prepare a bull as a sacrifice.

"Now ask your god to light the fire that will burn up your offering," Elijah told them.

They prayed and they danced around the altar they had built and they worked themselves into a frenzy... but nothing happened.

"Oh dear," said Elijah scornfully. "Perhaps Baal is asleep. Or maybe he's gone to the toilet."

Smiling to himself, Elijah walked over to another altar. It had been built for the worship of God and had fallen into ruin. He rebuilt the stonework. He piled up the firewood. He had another bull prepared as a sacrifice and laid on top. Finally, he ordered pitchers of water to be poured over everything.

Then Elijah prayed aloud: "O God, prove now that you are the God of Israel and that I am your servant."

God sent down a blaze of fire that consumed everything on the altar. ᧞

Not long after, a tiny rain cloud appeared in the sky. It grew and grew and billowed in the wind. As Elijah had predicted, the drought was over.

Jezebel was furious. "So Elijah made fools of my prophets and killed them. I'll have that troublemaker's blood for sure."

Elijah fled. Far away on the holy mountain of Sinai, God spoke to him. Ahab and Jezebel would suffer the consequences of their wickedness.

And so it turned out. Not long after, Ahab was killed in battle, dying slowly as his blood pooled on the floor of his chariot. His son Joram became king, but Elijah had already begun to put God's plan into action. He had sent a younger prophet, Elisha, to perform the ceremony of choosing another king: an ambitious army officer named Jehu.

The officer was a born leader. As he drove his chariot to a showdown with Joram, he easily won supporters. The king came out in his own chariot to confront the rebel.

"Do you come in peace?" Joram shouted.

"There can be no peace while your mother leads the nation astray with her false gods," replied Jehu. He fitted an arrow to his bow and shot Joram dead.

In her palace, Jezebel heard the grim news. She prepared herself in her finery and went to a high window in the palace to watch Jehu arrive.

On the holy mountain, God spoke to Elijah in a soft whisper of a voice.

I KINGS 19:12

"What have you come for?" she screamed down when she saw him.

Jehu looked up at the palace windows and simply shouted, "Who is on my side?"

At that, Jezebel's own servants threw her out of the window to her death. ✳

The Assyrian Invasion

Amos 5; 2 Kings 10, 17–20

✳

In the southern kingdom of Judah lived a shepherd named Amos. What he saw of life in the northern kingdom of Israel shocked him.

Make it your aim to do what is right, not what is evil. Then God really will be with you, as you claim he is.

Amos 5:14

Amos had not been raised to have grand ideas about himself. He was just a shepherd, a countryman. Those who had power or wealth or learning – well, they were in a different realm.

Yet when he visited the cities of Israel, what he saw of such people shocked him. He could not help but speak out.

"You people don't care about justice," he complained. "You don't care that you leave the poor with barely enough to eat. All you care about is building your fancy mansions and drinking wine from your private vineyards.

"You make life as hard as you can for those who are decent, honest, and hard-working. You break the law to get your own way and pay bribes to hush up the truth.

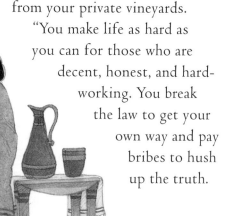

"Change your ways! Learn to do what is right... or you can be sure that God will allow you to be punished!"

But the kingdom seemed to be set on its own destruction. Even God's chosen king, Jehu, had not been able to keep the people obedient to God's laws. The nation became easy prey for its enemies. Of these, the most feared were the Assyrians, who were building an empire to the north.

For a while, the Assyrians merely demanded payment in return for staying out of Israel. Then one king refused to pay, and they invaded. The people of Israel were led away to live in other lands. Conquered peoples from other parts of the empire were settled in the land, known by the name of its city, Samaria. These new Samaritans were eager to worship the local deity, although the people of Judah could never accept that these foreigners could have anything to do with the God of Israel.

Over the years, the people of Judah had themselves failed to obey God's laws. At the time of the Assyrian invasion, however, King Hezekiah wanted his people to worship their own God faithfully. ॐ

Hezekiah was faithful to God and never disobeyed him, but carefully kept all the commands that God had given Moses.

2 KINGS 18:6

He refused to give in to the Assyrians. He
remained resolute even when the Assyrian army
laid siege to some of the principal cities in his
kingdom. Then, as one city after another fell,
he knew he had to act.

He sent a message to the Assyrian emperor. "Forgive me," he pleaded with the emperor. "Stop your attack and I will pay whatever you ask."

The emperor named his price, and Hezekiah even took gold and silver from the Temple so that he could pay.

It did no good. The emperor still sent his army to lay siege to Jerusalem. Hezekiah sent three officials to listen to what the Assyrian spokesperson had to say.

"Give in!" he cried. "Do you think we'd have come this far if your God had not sent us to destroy your wretched kingdoms?"

"Please speak your own language," urged Hezekiah's officials. "Don't use Hebrew as we do; our people are listening from the walls."

"So they are," said the Assyrian. He shouted aloud in Hebrew, "Don't let Hezekiah deceive you! If you surrender, our emperor will resettle you in a land every bit as good as this. If you fight, you'll die."

The people of Jerusalem listened in stunned silence. Even Hezekiah trembled at the thought of what lay ahead.

"I have made the best preparations I could," he explained to his advisors. "I have built an underground tunnel so that we can reach a spring of water, however long the siege lasts. But dare I hold out against such a powerful army?"

In desperation, Hezekiah sent messengers to the wisest prophet in Judah – a man named Isaiah.

Isaiah's response was confident and bold: "Don't be afraid of the Assyrians. God has allowed them victories, it is true; but God has promised to defend Jerusalem and protect it."

That night, without warning, death swept through the Assyrian camp.

The emperor was dismayed. "This disaster is a warning," he announced. "We must retreat at once."

For the rest of Hezekiah's reign, his people lived in peace, safe from enemy attack. *

God says this: "I will defend Jerusalem and protect it, for the sake of my own honour and because of the promise I made to David."

2 KINGS 19:34

THE STORY OF JONAH

JONAH 1–4

✳

THE ASSYRIANS HAD ALL BUT CRUSHED THE PEOPLE OF ISRAEL,
AND THE ISRAELITES HATED THEM. THE STORY OF JONAH
SUGGESTS THAT GOD HAD A DIFFERENT VIEW.

Long ago lived a prophet named Jonah. God
spoke to him, and gave very clear instructions:
"Go to Nineveh, the great city of Assyria. Warn
the people that I know how wicked they are."

"Warn the Assyrians," thought Jonah huffily.
"They don't deserve a warning. They deserve a
swift and brutal punishment."

He set off in quite the opposite direction. In
the port of Joppa, he asked if there were any ships
bound for Spain. When he found one, he agreed a
fare with the captain, got on board with the crew,
and found a cosy place below deck.

The ship set sail on the evening tide. Jonah was
rocked gently to sleep. He had escaped God's
calling.

In the night, God sent a violent storm. The wind
howled, the waves crashed, and the boat began to
take on water.

"Throw out the cargo," ordered the captain.
"Lighten the ship." Still the waves crashed over
the side and gurgled into the hold.

"The gods must be angry," wailed the sailors. "Let's draw lots to find out who is the cause of their anger."

Jonah was hauled on deck to take part in the choosing game. It pointed to him as the cause of the trouble.

"Sorry," he mumbled. "I'm running away from what God wants me to do."

The sailors howled at him. "That's a terrible thing to do. What can we do? We're bound to die."

Jonah looked out into the inky dark. He shrugged mournfully. "Throw me overboard," he said.

The sailors hesitated. "If we throw you to your death, we'll be punished," they complained. But the storm howled even louder and the boat lurched dangerously.

In desperation, they grabbed Jonah. "All you powers out there, we're sorry!" they cried. Then they threw Jonah to the waves. ❧

Jonah confessed, "I worship the Lord, the God of heaven, who made land and sea."

JONAH 1:9

The prophet went down, down, down into the
deep dark sea.

He held his breath, expecting to die as soon as he
gasped. He felt a sudden rush of water and then…
he breathed air. Jonah flailed his arms. It seemed
he was… inside something.

The hours passed… days perhaps. Jonah prayed
a desperate prayer:

"O God, I was in distress, and I called to you for help.
You threw me deep into the sea.
The seaweed wrapped itself around my head.
I was sinking into the land of no return.
And you heard me.
O God, If you save me,
I'll be your faithful and obedient servant for ever and ever.
I will do anything."

For a while, nothing happened. But then Jonah
felt himself being thrown forward.

The great sea creature – whatever it was – had
thrown him up onto a beach. Jonah could hardly
believe what had happened. He let himself be
washed clean of the creature's stench in the gently
lapping tide. Then he got up.

"I'm off to Nineveh," he called heavenward.
"I'll tell them all how wicked they are."

And so he did. When he reached the city, he
marched through it, calling his message. ❧

Jonah
prayed this:
"In my
distress,
O God,
I called to
you, and you
answered me."
Jonah 2:2

"Hear me! Change your ways, or God will destroy you. Forty days to turn to God. Hear me!"

The king heard the proclamation. He thought hard; then he made an amazing announcement: "That prophet – he's right! We must all change our ways at once. Everyone must dress in sackcloth to show their sorrow. That is an order."

The people didn't just obey their king. They saw just how bad they had been. They were genuinely sorry.

"Now I won't have to destroy them," said God.

Jonah was furious. "I knew you'd do that," he complained. "You let people off what they deserve at the slightest sign of sorrow. How does that make me look? How does that make me feel? I wish I were dead."

He went and built himself a little shelter on a hill overlooking the city. He could still watch and hope that something dreadful would happen to it.

The sun was hot. It beat down mercilessly. Then Jonah noticed a seed sprouting. It was growing before his eyes! As if by a miracle, its green leaves unfolded and cast a cool shadow.

"This makes life worth living again," said Jonah, and he smiled as he dozed.

The next day, God caused a worm to chew through the plant's stem. It wilted even more quickly than it had grown.

"My poor, lovely plant," Jonah complained to

The king of Nineveh said, "Everyone must pray earnestly to God and must give up their wicked behaviour and their evil actions."

JONAH 3:8

God. "Why did you let it be destroyed like that?"

For a long moment, there was silence. Jonah cast an angry look toward the heavens. More silence.

At last God spoke. "What right do you have to be angry about the plant? It grew in one night. You did nothing to make it grow… and yet you feel sorry for it.

"How much more, then, should I feel sorry for Nineveh. Think of the thousands of innocent children. Think of the animals." ✳

153

THE FALL OF JERUSALEM

2 KINGS 20–25

✳

THE KINGDOM OF JUDAH SURVIVED THE ASSYRIAN INVASION
AND STAYED INDEPENDENT FOR MANY YEARS. THEN THE
BABYLONIANS BEGAN AN EMPIRE OF THEIR OWN.

K ing Hezekiah was remembered as a good king.
He had trusted that God would help him
defy the Assyrians, and he believed that God had
brought him success.

The son who took the throne after him, and his
son in turn, did not follow his example. They set
up altars to other gods and worshipped at them,
forgetful of the covenant God had made with the
people.

Hezekiah's great-grandson Josiah was only eight
years old when the people made him their king. He
had been raised to obey God's laws and he did so
faithfully.

When he was a young man, he arranged for
building repairs to be made to the Temple. One
day, he sent a messenger to ask the high priest to
find out how much money had been put in the
collecting boxes so that the workers could be paid.

The messenger returned with a heavy scroll.
"The money has been paid as you asked," he said.
"While I was with the high priest, he asked me to

*Josiah followed
the example
of his ancestor
King David,
strictly obeying
all the laws of
God.*

2 KINGS 22:2

bring you this. It's something that's only just been found in all the upheaval."

He read what was written on the scroll. It was a very old copy of the book of the Law.

As Josiah listened, he became distraught. "There are so many laws that we have not known about," he said. "For generations we have not done the things that God commanded long ago."

He sent messengers to ask the advice of a wise woman – a prophet named Huldah.

"God is going to punish Jerusalem," she warned. "Its people have not been loyal in their worship.

"As for the king, he has shown how sorry he is for not having understood what the Law required. He will live out his life in peace." ❧

The prophet Huldah said, "God's anger is aroused against Jerusalem, and it will not die down."

2 KINGS 22:17

King Josiah summoned all the people and all the priests to a gathering at the Temple. There he read aloud from the book that set out the covenant made between God and the people so many years before. Everyone agreed that the entire nation must mend its ways.

Josiah began a zealous campaign: he ordered the immediate destruction of all the altars and shrines to foreign gods. He was dismayed to discover that there was a symbol of a foreign goddess inside the Temple; at once, he had it burned and the ash scattered over a burial ground.

When these reforms were complete, Josiah ordered the people to celebrate the Passover as described in the book of the covenant.

The kings who succeeded Josiah were far less strict in observing the Law, and the consequences of their wrongdoing were severe. First, the king of Egypt, to the south, harassed the people of Judah and demanded rich gifts in tribute. But there was worse to come.

The emperor of Babylon, King Nebuchadnezzar, had already defeated the Assyrians. Now he wanted to claim an even larger empire. When he came and besieged Jerusalem, the man who was king at the time surrendered. Nebuchadnezzar ordered him to go and live as a prisoner in Babylon. He also demanded that the royal officials and the most skilled workers be taken there as exiles. He seized all the golden utensils in the Temple and had them taken to his palace for his own use.

The agreement allowed the nation a brief time of peace. It might have continued, but the next king of Judah rebelled against Nebuchadnezzar. In response, the Babylonian army came and destroyed Jerusalem. Its houses, the royal palace, and the once-splendid Temple were burned to the ground. All the people, except for the poorest, were led away to Babylon. ✍

Bring us back to you, O Lord! Bring us back! Restore our ancient glory.

LAMENTATIONS 5:21

157

As for the golden ark of the covenant, it was taken from the Temple on the day of destruction and has never been seen since. ✳

THE FIERY FURNACE

DANIEL 1–3

IT WAS WHILE THE PEOPLE OF JUDAH WERE EXILES IN BABYLON
THAT THEY BECAME KNOWN AS THE JEWS.

When King Nebuchadnezzar defeated Judah, he took the nation's most talented people to Babylon. He asked his officials to choose from among them those who were handsome and healthy, intelligent, and quick to learn.

"Teach them to read and write the Babylonian language," he ordered. "I want to train these foreigners to serve in the royal court."

Among those chosen were Daniel and three others who were given the Babylonian names of Shadrach, Meshach, and Abednego. They were diligent in their studies and impressed everyone. However, they were determined to cling to their own traditions, choosing to eat just vegetables rather than eat meat that had not been prepared in accordance with their own Law.

In time, all the men took their place in government jobs. Daniel distinguished himself as someone who could interpret dreams and stayed in the royal court. Shadrach, Meshach, and Abednego were put in charge of provincial affairs.

One day, King Nebuchadnezzar had a gold statue

Daniel and his three friends, Shadrach, Meshach, and Abednego, impressed the king more than any of the others.

DANIEL 1:19

made: an idol of the great god of Babylon. It towered above the plain where it was erected. Then the king gave orders for all his officials to come together from all the provinces in his empire.

Once they were assembled, a herald made the announcement: "People of all nations, races, and languages, you are about to hear the sound of the festival orchestra. The music will begin with a great blast from the trumpets. There will follow a melody on the oboes, lyres, zithers, and harps. After that, all the other instruments will join in.

"As soon as the music starts, you are to bow down and worship this golden statue, as the great King Nebuchadnezzar has commanded. Anyone who does not obey will be deemed disloyal to the king. An awful punishment will swiftly follow: that person – or persons – will be cast into a blazing fiery furnace." ❧

The music rang out. The people bowed down;
except for three.

"Look," whispered a Babylonian official to
another. "Over there. Those Jewish men aren't
joining in the worship."

"At last," murmured the other. "I'm as furious as
you are at the way those foreigners are getting the
best jobs. Now we have a tale that will put an end
to their success."

They went to King Nebuchadnezzar and told
him of the disobedience of Shadrach, Meshach,
and Abednego.

The king flew into a rage. He summoned the
young men into his presence.

"I believed I could trust you to act responsibly,"

he cried. "My order was clear. At the sound of the music, you were supposed to bow to my golden statue. Yet I have been told that you refused to obey.

"Unless you agree to go and worship as you should, you will be thrown into the blazing fiery furnace. What god can save you then?"

When Shadrach, Meshach, and Abednego replied, their voices were calm and clear. "What you have heard about our conduct is true. We make no apology for what we did. If the God whom we serve can save us, then our God will."

King Nebuchadnezzar's face went red with anger. He barked his orders at a servant.

"Send orders for the furnace to be made seven times hotter," he said.

Then he turned to a guard. "Get the strongest men in the army to bind these men up right away and throw them into the flames," he snarled.

Everything was done swiftly and efficiently. King Nebuchadnezzar watched with a cruel smile as the guards dragged the three Jews to the furnace and hurled them in the heart of the fire. Indeed, the flames were so strong that the guards were burned up before they could run to safety. ❧

Give thanks to the Lord, for he is good and his mercy lasts for ever.

SONG OF THE THREE YOUNG MEN, VERSE 67

Suddenly Nebuchadnezzar leaped up.

"Three men — that's how many we threw into the furnace, is it not?"

"Yes, Your Majesty," the official replied.

"Then why do I see four?" asked the king. Slowly, fearfully, he returned his gaze to the fire.

"Look — four men walking about. They are not tied up. They are not hurt.

"And the fourth one... he looks like an angel."

The king went to the door of the furnace and shouted, "Shadrach, Meshach, Abednego — come out!"

The men came out. Their hair was not singed, their clothes were not scorched... they did not even smell of smoke.

"Praise the God of these three men!" cried Nebuchadnezzar. "They disobeyed me and risked their lives to keep his laws.

"There is no other god who is able to rescue people like this. Everyone should respect their God." ✳

DANIEL AND THE LIONS

DANIEL 2, 5–6

✳

THE STORIES OF DANIEL TELL OF GOD'S GREAT POWER
IN THE FACE OF PERSECUTION.

Daniel served as a high official in King
Nebuchadnezzar's court. God had given
him the gift of interpreting dreams, and the king
valued his wisdom and insight.

Even when Nebuchadnezzar died, Daniel
continued to serve in the royal palace. In time, a
man named Belshazzar came to the throne.

One night, King Belshazzar was holding a
banquet for a thousand of his noblemen. The
more they drank, the more rowdy and reckless they
became.

"I have an idea," said Belshazzar. "Let's get
those wonderful gold cups and bowls
our people took from the Temple in
Jerusalem. Our wives can drink out
of them while we drink toasts to
honour our gods."

As they did, a hand appeared
and began writing on the
wall. The king began to
shake with fear. "Find
someone who can read

these letters," he demanded. "It must be some prophecy."

The magicians and wizards were summoned, but they could not understand the writing. It was the queen mother who suggested that Daniel might be wiser than any of them.

He was brought to the banqueting hall where King Belshazzar was waiting.

"I served Nebuchadnezzar before I served you," said Daniel. "He came to see that he only held power when God allowed it. You do not honour God as you should. These are the words and their meaning:

"Number… for your days are numbered.

"Weight… for you lack the qualities of a king.

"Divisions… for your kingdom is going to be divided and given to the Medes and Persians."

That night, Darius the Mede seized power.

Like the Babylonian kings before him, Darius recognized Daniel's wisdom. He promoted him to high office, in charge of nearly all the other government officials. They, in turn, were very jealous.

"It's going to be hard to get rid of him," they agreed morosely. "We're not going to find any way to smear his character unless we find something to do with his religion. He's very earnest about it. Have you noticed how he goes off to his room to say prayers?" ❧

"It is God who gives wisdom and understanding. He knows what is hidden in darkness and is himself surrounded by light."

DANIEL'S PRAYER, DANIEL 2:21, 22

Then Daniel's enemies came up with a plan.
They went to King Darius.

"O King, may you live for ever," they said. "We have devised a law that will test the loyalty of everyone you rule.

"You should issue a decree that for thirty days, no one should be allowed to ask for anything from any god or human except you. That way, they will understand that all they have and all they can hope for depends on you and you alone.

"Warn them that anyone foolish enough to break that law will be thrown into a pit of lions."

King Darius was delighted. "A clever idea," he said. "The decree will be inescapable. As you know, a law of the Medes and Persians can never be altered."

Daniel heard about the new law. But he knew where his loyalties lay. He went to the room in his house that faced Jerusalem. There he prayed to God, as he did three times a day.

Daniel's enemies raced off to tell the king. "We have bad news," they said, trying to hide their joy. "Your servant Daniel has disobeyed you. In spite of the new law, he is still saying prayers to his own God."

Darius frowned. "The law wasn't intended for Daniel," he said. "I know he's loyal."

"But you cannot change a law of the Medes and Persians," urged Daniel's enemies. "That's… that's the law."

The king saw he was trapped. Glowering at his officials, he gave orders for Daniel to be taken to the pit where the lions prowled.

"I can only hope your God rescues you," he murmured to Daniel as he was hustled past.

King Darius spent a sleepless night.

"No, I don't want food," he snapped at his servants, "and I don't want a drink and I shall fire the lot of you if anyone suggests that I might like the musicians to come and play to me."

There was only one thing on his mind. What was happening in the pit of lions? At first light, he hurried over.

"Daniel," he called hesitantly. "Are you all right?" ❧

Daniel did not do anything wrong or dishonest.

Daniel 6:4

"I'm very well," called Daniel cheerfully. "God sent an angel to watch over me, and the lions haven't even opened their mouths."

Darius was overjoyed. He gave orders for Daniel to be pulled out of the pit.

"Your God is the living god," he declared. "Your God performs wonders and miracles.

"As for those who planned your death… Guard, throw them to the lions!" ✳

QUEEN ESTHER

ESTHER 1–9

✳

THE PERSIAN EMPIRE SPREAD FAR AND WIDE. SOON THERE
WERE COMMUNITIES OF JEWS IN MANY DIFFERENT PLACES.
THIS STORY IS OF THAT TIME.

When the Persians took control, people were able to travel fairly freely through the empire. Soon there were communities of Jews in many different places.

Long ago, King Xerxes ruled from his palace in Persia's capital city of Susa. Although he could be generous, he was also feared: whatever he ordered had to be obeyed throughout the vast empire, and he had power of life and death over all his subjects.

One day, his wife, the beautiful Queen Vashti, refused to come to his summons. Xerxes was furious not to get his own way. He made plans to choose a new wife.

Officials were sent throughout the empire to search for the most beautiful girls of marriageable age. Among those they chose was an orphaned Jew named Esther. She had been raised by her cousin Mordecai. He was very proud of his background, having lived in Jerusalem before the Babylonians destroyed it.

Mordecai had lots of last-minute advice for Esther as she prepared to go to the palace. "Remember you're a Jew," he told her, "but at the same time, don't tell anyone. Lots of people are prejudiced against us, and that could spell trouble."

For a whole year, all the chosen girls were given beauty treatments and prepared for the role of queen. Then Xerxes made his choice... and Esther was his favourite. He declared a holiday throughout the empire to honour the day he made her his new queen.

Meanwhile, Mordecai had been given a government job. From his office in the palace, he overheard a plot to assassinate King Xerxes. He managed to send a message to Esther, who, in turn, told the king.

Xerxes ordered an investigation. The plot was uncovered and the traitors were put to death.

"These events should go down in history," declared Xerxes. "Make a written report and be sure to include all the details."

Life in the palace returned to normal. Some time later, King Xerxes chose a man named Haman to be prime minister.

Xerxes made a formal announcement. "I want all my officials and government workers to bow down to my chosen deputy to show their loyalty."

Everyone obeyed, except for Mordecai. ❧

"I am a Jew," he explained to his fellow workers. "My faith forbids me to bow down to anyone."

When Haman found out that Mordecai was a Jew, he was furious. Haman was descended from the Amalekites – a tribe who had for hundreds of years been the sworn enemies of Mordecai's people.

He went to the king. "There is an entire race living in your empire who are by nature evil," he lied. "They are disloyal and rebellious. But I have a solution that will put an end to the trouble they represent.

"Simply name a day on which all loyal subjects will have a duty to kill any Jew they know."

Haman bowed low and smiled unctuously. Xerxes was delighted to have an advisor who was so diligent. He totally believed Haman's lies and passed the law.

As soon as Mordecai heard, he sent a message to Esther. Surely she could plead with the king not to allow her people to be massacred!

"The king hasn't asked to see me in weeks," Esther wept. "To go to him unasked for can be punished by death."

She sent a message back asking him to tell all the Jews to pray for her. She herself spent three days praying. Then she dressed in her royal robes and went and stood where the king could see her from his throne room.

The king looked up, first indignant, then smiling. He gave the sign that she could come nearer. "What can I do for you?" he asked.

"Please, Your Majesty," said Esther. "I would like you and Haman to come to a banquet."

The king agreed, and the banquet was a great success. All Esther asked for was that the two men should come for another banquet the following evening. ✌

Haman went home in an excellent mood... until he saw Mordecai as he hurried along. The Jew showed him no respect, which put him in a temper. He immediately ordered his servants to arrange for a gallows to be built. "I'll hang the scoundrel myself," he told his wife.

As for the king – he could not sleep that night. To help pass the time, he asked for some of the official records to be read aloud to him. He listened to the account of how Mordecai had foiled a plot. "That decent, loyal man was never given the praise due to him," he said. "I must ask Haman's advice about how to honour a national hero."

When Haman heard the king's question next morning, he could not believe how well things were going. If the king wanted to honour someone... well, it could only be him.

"Dress the man in royal robes," said Haman. "Have him ride through the city streets while a high official leads the way."

"That's perfect," said the king. "Do that for Mordecai today, please."

Only the prospect of a second private banquet with Esther and the king kept Haman from feeling utterly humiliated as he carried out the task. The banquet was a pleasant relief... delightful, in fact.

The mood was rosy as Esther made her request.

"Your Majesty," she said, "I need your help: an enemy is plotting my people's destruction."

"An outrage," replied Xerxes. "And who is this wicked enemy?"

"It may surprise you," said Esther. She paused. "It's that man there: the unspeakable Haman."

The king was furious. How many wicked people had wormed their way into his service? He left the room to collect his thoughts. When he returned, he found Haman clutching at Esther, pleading with her.

"Take your hands off my wife!" shouted the king, clenching his fists.

One of the servants, wanting to direct the king's rage, stepped forward. "There is a gallows ready, Your Majesty: one that Haman built for Mordecai."

"Hang Haman on it," the king ordered.

The planned massacre of the Jews did not take place. On Xerxes' orders, the day chosen for their destruction became the day they defeated their enemies. ✳

Rebuilding Jerusalem

Ezra 1–4; Zechariah 9; Nehemiah 1–9

✳

In the year that Cyrus of Persia became emperor, he allowed all the people who had been made exiles by the Babylonians to return to their homeland.

God said, "In order to show the many nations that I am holy, I will bring my people back from all the countries where their enemies live."

Ezekiel 39:27

The day came when the Jews who had been taken to Babylon were allowed to go back home. They longed to rebuild the Temple in Jerusalem. Indeed, the Persians allowed them to take with them some of the gold and silver treasures that had been looted from it years before. Even so, it was the people themselves who put their own money into a rebuilding fund and set to work.

When the time came for the foundation to be laid, they began with songs of worship. The priests played the ceremonial trumpets and the musicians clashed the cymbals. Some shouted for joy; others, who had seen the first Temple burned, wept with emotion.

In spite of everyone's eagerness, there were problems. Judah had not been empty during the exile. The people who had been living there offered to share the work. The Jews declined the offer, not wanting outside interference. Soon there was bad feeling, and fights broke out.

It was not just the building work that proved challenging. It was just as hard to rebuild the traditions of the faith and to celebrate the festivals as the Law required.

A prophet named Zechariah gave them hope.

"Be joyful," he told them. "A new king is going to come. He will be a king of peace, who rides a donkey and not a warhorse.

"He will save his people, as a shepherd saves his flock from danger."

Meanwhile, there remained many Jews throughout the empire who had not gone back to Jerusalem. Among them was a man named Nehemiah. He was eager to hear news of the rebuilding… and disappointed by what he heard. He could not hide his sadness one day, when he was going about his job, serving wine at the table of the emperor Artaxerxes. ❧

God says this: "I will make my people strong; they will worship and obey me."

ZECHARIAH 10:12

The emperor noticed. "You're not ill, are you?" he enquired. "You do look miserable. Whatever is the matter?"

Nehemiah was startled. "Oh, Your Majesty! I was just thinking about my people's city, Jerusalem. I hear it is still a ruin in spite of the efforts of those that are resettling it."

"What a pity," said the emperor. "Is there anything you want to do about it?"

Nehemiah said the swiftest of prayers before he answered. "Your Majesty, would you allow me to leave your service and go to Jerusalem in person?"

The emperor agreed. He even gave Nehemiah an armed escort for the journey. However, when Nehemiah reached Jerusalem, he took care not to announce himself.

One night, he got on his donkey and rode around the broken walls. What he saw helped him decide what to do.

As soon as he could, he went to the leaders of the city. "We must rebuild the walls," he said. "That will restore pride in our city."

Nehemiah was efficient at organizing the work. The local people who were not Jewish once again complained. "You'll never make anything out of that rubble," they laughed. "That wall you're working on – a fox could knock it down." ❧

Everyone knew that the work had been done with God's help.

NEHEMIAH 6:16

"The Lord is good, and his love for Israel is eternal."

EZRA 3:11

As the work progressed, so the opposition grew. Nehemiah found out that some of the locals were planning to attack, so he made a plan: half of the workforce would stand guard while the others actually did the building. Everyone would have a weapon handy, just in case.

It was a triumph. In just a few weeks, the walls were complete. Now people could come and live in the city believing they were safe. In the surrounding towns too, the Jews felt they were putting down roots.

They set a day to gather in Jerusalem so they could all listen as a priest named Ezra read to them from the book of the Law. As they listened, the mood changed. "We keep falling far short of what God wants," they said. "God has brought us back to our land. Surely we can live as God's people here?"

"Don't be sad," said Ezra. "Tomorrow we celebrate a festival. We must all build shelters of branches, to remember when we lived as nomads in the time of Moses. During the days of the festival, we will all hear a portion of the Law read aloud. Then we will have a day of saying sorry to God... and we will make a new start." ✳

The Time of Jesus

Little more than four hundred years passed from the time of the Jews returning from exile in a foreign land to the birth of Jesus.

Exile had transformed the Jewish faith. It was now firmly centred on the Law that had been given in the time of Moses. There was also great respect for the sayings of other prophets, and these too began to be gathered into the collection of Scriptures.

Additionally, the Jews had begun the custom of meeting on the sabbath day each week. The meeting places were called synagogues. An important part of each meeting was hearing a portion of the Scriptures read aloud. Some men took on the role of teacher – rabbi – within the synagogue. The rabbis also set up schools in their communities to teach young boys to read. As grown-ups, they would be able to take their turn reading aloud to the community.

Many rabbis were also Pharisees. The word means "separated ones". Pharisees believed that keeping the Law was at the heart of what it meant to be Jewish. From the Scriptures, they identified 613 commandments. Of these, 248 were things obedient Jews must do, and 365 were things obedient Jews must not do.

Although the Jewish faith was strong, the Jewish nation was far from powerful. The Persian empire that ruled over it was defeated by a young Greek commander named

Alexander. He ruled over even more lands, including the land of the Jews. They, in turn, were angry as Greek customs and beliefs were forced upon them.

Later, the Romans became the world superpower. In 63 BCE, a Roman general named Pompey conquered Jerusalem and even marched into the Temple. The Romans put governors in charge of the different provinces of their empire. After some years, the person chosen to be in charge in Jerusalem was a ruthless man named Herod. He was even given the title "king of the Jews". He was not a godly man, but, both to show how powerful he was and to impress his Jewish subjects, he ordered a beautiful new Temple to be built in Jerusalem.

It was this Herod who was king when Jesus was born. It was Herod's Temple that Jesus visited.

Through all this period, the Jewish people longed to be a great nation again. One prophet after another promised that God would send them a king like David.

"The royal line of David is like a tree that has been cut down," declared the prophet Isaiah, "but just as new branches sprout from a stump, so a new king will arise from among David's descendants....

"He will know the Lord's will and honour him,
and find pleasure in obeying him."

Isaiah 11:2–3

The title that the Jews gave this longed-for king was "messiah". The Greek version of the word was "christ".

THE BIRTH OF JESUS

MATTHEW 1–2; LUKE 1–2

✳

THE STORIES OF THE BIRTH OF JESUS ARE FOUND IN THE
GOSPELS OF MATTHEW AND LUKE. THEY PAY TRIBUTE TO THE
BELIEF THAT JESUS IS THE CHRIST AND THE SON OF GOD.

*The angel said
to Mary, "Peace
be with you! The
Lord is with you
and has greatly
blessed you!"*

LUKE 1:28

In the time when Herod ruled the land of the
Jews, there lived a priest named Zechariah. One
day, he was taking his turn in the worship service
at the Temple. While the people prayed in the
courtyards beyond, he was burning incense in the
dark interior.

Suddenly, he gasped. There, among the curls of
smoke, was an angel: Gabriel.

"Don't be afraid," said the angel. "I bring news
that you and your wife, Elizabeth, are going to
have a son. You will name him John. He will be a
prophet, and his preaching will call many back to
God."

Zechariah was astonished. He was
also disbelieving – for he and his wife
were both quite old; but not long after
he returned home, his wife did indeed
become pregnant.

Then, in the sixth month of
Elizabeth's pregnancy, God
sent Gabriel to Nazareth,

to a young woman named Mary.

Mary too was startled to see the angel.

"Please don't be afraid," said Gabriel. "I bring news of God's great blessing. You will give birth to a son: Jesus. He will be known as the Son of the Most High God. He will be a king like David, of days gone by, and his kingdom will never end."

Mary almost laughed. "I may be engaged to Joseph," she said, "but I'm not yet married. I can't possibly be pregnant!"

"This will happen because of God," replied Gabriel. "There is nothing God cannot do. Remember your cousin Elizabeth; she is expecting a baby, and no one believed that would ever happen."

"I will do as God wants," said Mary softly.

She was eager to tell Elizabeth her news – who else dared she tell? – and her cousin believed all she said about the angel's message.

When Joseph first heard Mary's news, he was dismayed. Then, in a dream, an angel spoke to him. "Take care of Mary and her child," said the angel, "for he is God's Son." Joseph believed the angel and agreed to marry Mary. When the Roman emperor ordered a census, he asked Mary to travel to his hometown of Bethlehem to register there. ❧

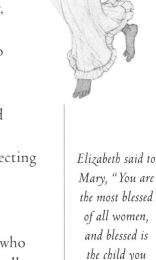

Elizabeth said to Mary, "You are the most blessed of all women, and blessed is the child you will bear!"

LUKE 1:42

They arrived weary from several days' journey. Joseph enquired of his relatives where they might stay, but returned with dismay written over his face.

"No one has any room for us," he explained. "All we've been offered is a stable."

There, where ox and ass munched and shuffled, Mary's baby was born. She wrapped him in swaddling clothes and laid him in a manger.

On the hillsides nearby, shepherds were sitting out under the stars, taking care of their sheep. Suddenly, one of God's angels appeared, shining with all the splendour of heaven.

"Don't be afraid," said the angel. "I bring good news for you and all the world. Tonight, in Bethlehem, a baby has been born. He is cradled in a manger… but do not be misled by the humble surroundings. For the child is God's chosen king – the messiah, the Christ."

At that moment, a great company of angels appeared, singing praises to God. Then they vanished into the dark vault of the heavens.

The hillside was silent but for the bleating of sleepy sheep and the rustling of leaves. Then a shepherd boy cried, "Come on! Let's go and see if what we have heard is true."

The shepherds hurried to Bethlehem and found Mary and Joseph and the baby in the manger. ও

The angels sang these words: "Glory to God in the highest heaven, and peace on earth to those with whom he is pleased!"

LUKE 2:14

In nearby Jerusalem, some travellers were making enquiries. "We have come from lands to the east," they explained. "We study the night sky, and we have seen a new star: a sign that a new king has been born to the Jews. Its light has led us here"

When the news reached the royal palace, Herod scowled. "The Roman emperor gave *me* the title of king," he said. He went to consult his advisors.

"Oh yes," they told him. "Many prophets spoke of God sending a king – a messiah. One declared that he would be born in Bethlehem – the same place as King David was born, you know."

"Bring those foreigners here," said Herod.

By the light of flickering lamps, he listened to what the wise men had to say. "Go to Bethlehem," he said. "Find out all you can about this newborn king. Then come and tell me."

He leaned forward, smiling faintly. "I should like to go and pay my respects to the true king of my people," he said. "But I want my arrival to be... a surprise for the family."

As the travellers started out for Bethlehem, the star they had followed all the way to Jerusalem still shone on their way. In the hilltop town, it stopped and twinkled merrily over one small house.

The wise men went inside and found the child with his mother, Mary. They brought out their gifts: gold, frankincense, and myrrh.

The following morning was overcast. A chill wind blew.

"We're troubled by the way Herod spoke," the wise men agreed. "Let's go home another way – without visiting him."

In the night, fears had come to Joseph too.

"Mary," he said gently. "In my dream, an angel spoke to me. I am afraid King Herod will come looking for the child. Let us hurry to where he cannot harm us."

So the little family gathered up all they had and went to Egypt. ✳

JESUS GROWS UP

LUKE 2

✳

SOME TIME AFTER JESUS' BIRTH, WHEN KING HEROD WAS DEAD,
JOSEPH DECIDED IT WAS SAFE TO TAKE HIS FAMILY TO NAZARETH.
THERE JESUS GREW UP.

Every year, Jesus' parents used to go to
Jerusalem for the Passover. It was the dream
of every Jew to be at the Temple for this, the most
important festival of all.

Passover was the time to recall the story of
Moses and how, long ago, he had led the people
out of slavery in Egypt. It was the time to reflect
on the laws that Moses had given the people from
God – the laws at the heart of their
ancient covenant. It was time to
recall the covenant promise that,
by obeying the Law, God would
be their God and they would be
God's people.

When Jesus was twelve, his
parents allowed him to join
them. By that age, like all the
boys, he had spent several
years learning about the
Jewish faith at the
synagogue school.

He could read fluently from the Scriptures. Jesus' parents were confident that he would treat the pilgrimage seriously.

At the same time, the trip was also a holiday. Many in Nazareth looked forward to going to Jerusalem each spring. They journeyed together – a noisy, chattering group of pilgrims wending their way along the stony road and gathering each night to share food and stories.

Once in Jerusalem, they went to the Temple together to take part in the prayers and the special worship services. They marvelled too at the progress on the building: King Herod himself had ordered the construction of a splendid new Temple – gleaming white stone, decked with gold and surrounded by a wide courtyard with elegant colonnades.

All too soon, the week of celebration was over, and the entire group from Nazareth set off on the long journey home. Some strode out purposefully, others walked more steadily, and yet others were taking even longer, fussing over their belongings and all the complications of the trip.

"And where do you suppose Jesus is?" Mary complained to a relative as she hurried along, struggling with a heavy bag. "I haven't seen him since this morning." ✍

Moses said this to the people: "Today the Lord your God has accepted you as his own people, as he promised you; and he commands you to obey all his laws."

DEUTERONOMY 26:18

"Honour the Lord your God by celebrating Passover in the month of Abib; it was on a night in that month that he rescued you from Egypt."

DEUTERONOMY 16:1

193

"Oh, those youngsters — aren't they the limit!" came the reply. "I saw a group of them daring each other to run the whole way. We'll probably find them slumped by the roadside complaining they're worn out."

They didn't. When the pilgrims from Nazareth met by a roadside inn that evening, Mary marched over to where the young people were lounging and laughing.

"Where's Jesus?" she asked.

"Don't know," was all the reply she got, along with a few shrugs and grimaces.

Mary went to ask the family of some of Jesus' friends. They hadn't seen him either. In fact, no one had.

Suddenly, Mary felt herself going cold with fear. "We'll have to go back," she told her husband. "Let's start now… while there's still some light. We must find him."

As she hurried back to Jerusalem, her mind filled with a hundred and one horrible things that might have befallen her son.

The following day, when they reached the city, they went back to all the places they had been together. They asked all the shopkeepers they had bought things from. They asked beggars who still sat patiently on the same corners as before and even soldiers who patrolled the streets.

On the third day, they went around all the same places yet again. In the colonnade of the Temple, they saw him. ❧

Jesus was sitting with the religious teachers, debating in lively fashion like a true scholar. The older men were smiling and nodding approvingly as Jesus explained his opinions.

"A highly original point of view," one was saying. "And very convincing."

"Where have you been?" Mary almost screamed as she rushed to hug him. "We've been so worried about you!" And then she began to laugh and cry at the same time.

"Why did you have to look?" replied Jesus. "Didn't you know that I had to be in my Father's house?"

He stood up and waved to the teachers. "Time to go!" he said cheerfully. "I'm really glad I came."

Then Jesus went back to Nazareth. As he grew to be a young man, he was diligent in learning the family trade and obedient to his devoted mother. ✳

Jesus grew both in body and in wisdom, gaining favour with God and people.

LUKE 2:52

JESUS AND THE CHOICE

MATTHEW 3–4; MARK 1; LUKE 3–4; JOHN 1

✳

THE ACCOUNTS OF JESUS' LIFE IN THE BIBLE FOCUS ON THE TIME
WHEN HE LEFT HIS WORK AS A CARPENTER IN NAZARETH AND
CHOSE TO BECOME A PREACHER.

*Zechariah said
to John, "You,
my child, will be
called a prophet
of the Most
High God. You
will... tell his
people that they
will be saved by
having their sins
forgiven."*

LUKE 1:76–77

Jesus' cousin John was a striking figure. Anyone who came to see him – out in the wild country beside the River Jordan – might have thought they had stepped back in time; for John had the appearance of a prophet from ancient times.

He was lean from frugal living, dark from the sun, with an abundance of untrimmed hair. His clothes were made from coarsely woven camel hair and secured around his waist by a leather belt. When he preached, his voice was powerful.

"Turn away from all your wrongdoing!" he cried. "Come, and I will baptize you right here in the River Jordan to show your commitment. As I plunge you beneath the water, it will be like dying to your old ways. As I lift you up, it will be like rising to a new life."

Many were convinced, and every day more pilgrims came to be baptized and to rededicate themselves to living in obedience to God.

Others came out of curiosity: to gawp, to laugh, to mock.

"You snakes," he roared at them. "Do you think you can escape God's punishment? You know only too well how crooked and corrupt you are. You know how you have flouted every good law and tradition.

"God's axe is ready, and every one of you is a tree in his orchard. Has your life produced a harvest of good deeds? If not, then beware. Like a barren tree, you will be cut down.

"Change your ways now, while there is still time. Get ready to meet God when he comes in person."

Soon, even the most cynical listeners were glancing nervously at one another.

"What are we supposed to do?" they wanted to know.

"Think about all your possessions," said John. "How many spare sets of clothes do you have? Stop your wasteful spending and give to those who have nothing. And how much food do you gobble down each day? Could you not share with those who face hunger and starvation?" ❧

John reminded his listeners of what the prophet Isaiah said: "Someone is shouting in the desert: 'Get the road ready for the Lord; make a straight path for him to travel!'"

LUKE 3:4,
QUOTING
ISAIAH 40:3

John listened gravely to some tax collectors who had come to ask for special advice. "You know the difficulties of the work we do," they began. "We collect the money the Roman government demands from everyone, and just a little more for our own payment. We don't get proper wages."

"Then stick to collecting the legal amount," replied John bluntly. "That's you dealt with easily enough! Now, what are these soldiers wanting to know?"

The soldiers were part of the Roman army – foreigners mainly. They had only come to police the crowds, but John's message had made them feel guilty for all their casual brutality.

"You can do your job in an honest way," he told them. "Don't accuse the innocent of wrongdoing. Don't use force to make people give you money. Be content with your pay."

People were impressed by John's teaching. "Perhaps he is the messiah," they began to say. "Perhaps he will be the king who will make us God's own people again."

John heard the rumour and dismissed it.

"Someone much greater is coming," he said robustly. "I can baptize you with water. He will baptize you with the Holy Spirit. God will sort the good from the bad, just like a farmer winnows his crop. The grain will be gathered safely into his barn, and the chaff tossed on a fire."

Then, to his amazement, John saw his cousin, who had come all the way from Galilee. It was Jesus, and he was asking to be baptized.

John shook his head. "You have nothing to repent of," he said. "You should be baptizing me."

Jesus insisted that his baptism would mark the start of his new calling. At last, John agreed, and as he lifted Jesus out of the water, he saw God's Holy Spirit come down and settle on him in the form of a dove. He heard a voice from heaven saying, "You are my own dear Son. I am pleased with you." ❧

After that, Jesus went off alone into the barren and remote hill country. For forty days he ate nothing, and hunger began to gnaw at him.

The devil came along with a tempting idea. "If you are God's Son, you could order this stone to turn into bread."

Jesus had learned the Scriptures well. "It is written," he replied, "that life is about more than bread."

Then the devil made another suggestion. "Look! In your mind's eye, can you see the kingdoms of the world? Live by my standards; worship me. Then they will all be yours."

"But," said Jesus, "the Scriptures say this: 'Worship the Lord your God and serve only him.'"

A third time, the devil came to tempt Jesus. "Imagine!" he said. "You are on the highest point of the Temple in Jerusalem. The crowds are watching… waiting. You throw yourself off the edge… and God sends angels to keep you from harm. What a miracle! What a demonstration of your exalted status!"

But Jesus simply said, "The Scriptures say, 'Do not put the Lord your God to the test.'"

Then the devil knew that Jesus could not be tempted away from his calling, so he left him… for a while. ✳

JESUS AND THE FISHERMEN

MATTHEW 4, 8, 13; MARK 1, 6; LUKE 4–5

✳

JESUS HAD CHOSEN TO FOLLOW GOD'S CALLING AND BECOME
A PREACHER. IT WAS QUITE USUAL FOR LOCAL SYNAGOGUES TO
INVITE VISITING PREACHERS.

*Jesus taught in
the synagogues
and was praised
by everyone.*

LUKE 4:15

Jesus was determined to follow his new calling.
He did not go back to the family trade in
Nazareth, where he was known as the carpenter's
son. Instead, he went to one of the synagogues in
the area and introduced himself as a preacher.

His words were well received, and invitations
came from other synagogues. News of his
popularity had reached the ears of the townsfolk
of Nazareth when, at last, he returned there.

On the sabbath, Jesus went to the synagogue
as usual. He was asked to read the Scriptures for
the day, and was handed the book of the prophet
Isaiah. He stood at the reading desk, unrolled the
scroll, and began.

*"The spirit of the Lord is upon me,
because he has chosen me to bring good news to the poor.
He has sent me to proclaim liberty to the captives
and recovery of sight to the blind;
to set free the oppressed
and announce that the time has come
when the Lord will save his people."*

It was a striking passage. The people watched in silence as Jesus handed back the scroll and went to sit down. He looked up at them and said, "This passage of the Scriptures has come true today, as you heard it being read."

The remark prompted whispering and murmuring. "Isn't he simply the son of Joseph?"

"He is – but haven't you heard of the miracles he's been working in other towns? Perhaps he'll show us one right here."

Jesus spoke above the chatter. "I know what kinds of things you're saying," he said. "But just remember the stories from the Scriptures: none of the prophets were welcome in their own town."

"Oh – so you think you're a prophet now, do you?" shouted a man. "I've known you for years, you arrogant young man!"

"Your claim is ridiculous," agreed the rest. "We're not having you talk this nonsense in our synagogue!"

In an instant, the congregation became a mob. They dragged Jesus out of town to a well-known precipice on the hillside.

"Who wants to help throw him off?" came the cry.

But in the moment's pause before anyone could act, Jesus simply walked through the middle of the crowd and down the road. ❧

"I tell you this," said Jesus. "Prophets are never welcomed in their home town."

LUKE 4:24

On the shores of Lake Galilee, the people of Capernaum were pleased to have the young preacher in their midst. They willingly invited him to speak in their synagogue.

A man sat in the corner, mumbling to himself. Everyone was used to the fact that he lived in a troubled world of his own. Suddenly, he shouted, "What do you want with us, Jesus of Nazareth? Are you here to destroy us? I know who you are: you are God's holy messenger."

Jesus gazed at the man sternly. "Evil spirit, be quiet," he said.

The man fell to the ground with a cry... but then stood up. Everyone stared as he went back quietly to his place. Whatever had troubled him was gone. By a miracle.

At the end of the service, a young fisherman named Simon came up to Jesus.

"I've heard how the good people of Nazareth treated you," he said. "Come and stay with me. My mother-in-law isn't well, but you'll still be made welcome."

Jesus went to Simon's house, and with a word cured the older woman of her fever. At once, she was able to bustle around organizing her household... and to tell her neighbours of what had happened. By the evening, news of her astonishing recovery had spread. All those with friends who were sick brought them to Jesus. He healed them all.

The next day, Jesus went off again to preach in other synagogues in Galilee. By the time he returned to Capernaum, he was a local hero. Crowds gathered by the water's edge, eager to listen to all he had to say. Jesus saw Simon's boat. He climbed on board and asked his friend to push the boat into shallow water. From there, he preached all day.

When the crowd had gone, he spoke to Simon. "You and your partners, take the two boats out further and let the nets down."

"It's not worth it," responded Simon gloomily. "We fished all night and caught nothing."

Then he looked at Jesus' expression. "Oh, if you want, we can," he said.

The men let their net drift, then pulled it into a circle. To their amazement, it was full to breaking. The men struggled to bring their catch to shore. ✍

Jesus went to Galilee and preached the Good News from God. "The right time has come," he said, "and the kingdom of God is near! Turn away from your sins and believe the Good News!"

MARK 1:14–15

"Don't be alarmed," said Jesus. "From now on, I want you to join me in a new venture. You will be fishing for people... gathering together those who want to follow me."

Simon and his brother Andrew pulled up one boat. James and his brother John pulled up the other. They left everything to follow Jesus. ✳

MIRACLES AND MURMURS

MATTHEW 8–9, 12; MARK 1–2; LUKE 5–6

✳

JESUS' MIRACLES OF HEALING MADE HIM HUGELY POPULAR.
HOWEVER, THE RELIGIOUS AUTHORITIES WERE SUSPICIOUS
OF ALL HE SAID AND DID.

In the time of Jesus, those who were sick had little hope of cure. There was one dreaded skin disease that left its victims horribly disfigured. For this, they were shunned by their communities.

One day, a man who suffered this condition came and flung himself at Jesus' feet.

"I know you could make me well," he sobbed. "Surely you want to help me?"

Jesus reached out and touched him. "Of course I want to help," he said. "May you be completely free of your disease."

The cure was sudden and dramatic. "This is… amazing!" cried the man. "I can't tell you how much this means to me. My old friends are going to be astonished. I can't wait to tell them."

"Wait a moment," said Jesus quietly. "I don't want you to make a big show of what has happened. Just go to the priest and ask him to examine you.

If he gives you a clean bill of health, you will be able rejoin your community without further ado."

In spite of Jesus' request, the news of the healing spread. Crowds of people came to ask Jesus to heal them. He was not given a moment's peace whenever he arrived in a community.

The religious authorities were also interested in what Jesus was doing. They knew that his preaching was popular... but was it faithful to the Scriptures? One group, the Pharisees, were zealous about making sure that even the smallest details of the religious laws were understood. They were eager to question Jesus more closely.

An opportunity came when someone made his house available for a meeting. Rabbis and Pharisees came to Capernaum from as far away as Jerusalem to talk with Jesus there. In no time at all, crowds had gathered outside in the hope of seeing a miracle.

"So that's bad news for us then!" exclaimed a group of young men. They had a friend who was paralysed, and they had carried him as far as the house using his sleeping mat as a stretcher but could not get near the door.

For a moment, they sat glumly while yet more arrivals almost trampled over them. Then one spoke. ❧

Jesus would go away to lonely places, where he prayed.

Luke 5:16

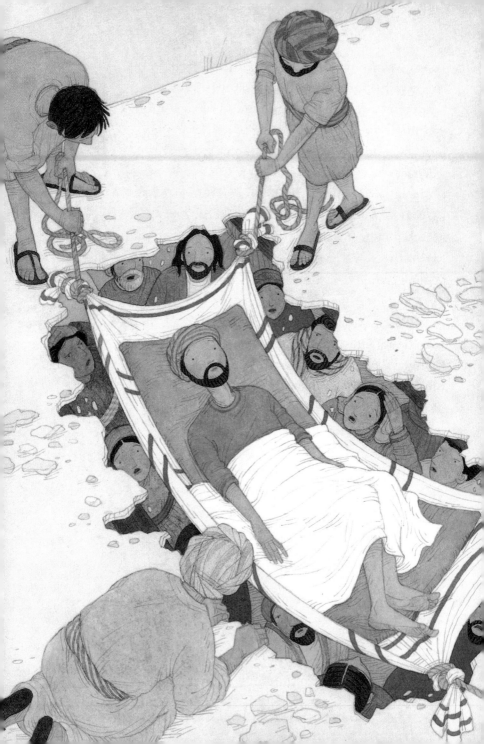

"We can use the outside stairs to get to the roof," he said. "It's easy to break through to the room below — between the roof beams are just branches and mud plaster. We can fix it afterwards."

They set to work. They could hardly stop themselves laughing as they saw disapproving faces gazing up at them — except for one. Did Jesus give a wink of amusement? Then they fixed ropes to their friend's mat and lowered him into the room.

"Well, your friends obviously think I can help you," said Jesus to the man. "Your sins are forgiven, my friend."

"What did he say?" the Pharisees whispered. "It's totally wrong for Jesus to say that. It's blasphemy. Only God can forgive sins!"

"Which is easier to say?" Jesus asked them. " 'Your sins are forgiven' or 'Get up and walk'? I will show you that I speak with authority."

He turned to the paralysed man. "This is what I want you to do," he said. "Get on your feet, roll up that bed mat, and go home."

The man looked anxious for just a moment. Then he cautiously pushed himself to a sitting position. To cheers from above, he got to his feet, grabbed his mat, and gave a shout of joy.

The crowd drew back in astonishment to let the man dance his way outdoors. ❧

Jesus also got up and went off down the street to the marketplace. A man named Levi was at his booth there, collecting taxes for the Romans.

"I want you as one of my followers," said Jesus. "Come now."

Levi stood up and went. "I can't believe you chose me," he said to Jesus, smiling broadly. "Those religious types have written me off as the enemy – you know, collaborating with the Romans. But you believe I could be someone worthwhile. I'm going to have a party to celebrate this."

The religious leaders were still discussing the incident with the same man when they heard about the tax collector's party. As soon as they could, they sent a delegation to complain.

"It's quite wrong," they told Jesus, "to eat and drink with the likes of Levi and his tax-collector friends. That's not proper behaviour for anyone who claims to be a man of God."

"I haven't come to call respectable people to be friends of God," said Jesus. "My message is for those who are ready to admit their wrongdoing."

His reply provoked rage. The people who were suspicious of Jesus soon began a whispering campaign against him.

"It's one thing after another," the Pharisees complained. "We saw his band of followers picking grain on the sabbath. They were rubbing out the kernels and popping them in their mouths. That's harvesting on the day of rest."

"In my synagogue," said a rabbi, "Jesus actually called a man to the front and healed his paralysed hand on the sabbath. That's work too. And he as good as said that God would have wanted that because it was a good deed."

"That Jesus is trouble," they agreed. "We must stop him." ✳

Jesus asked this of his critics: "What does our Law allow us to do on the sabbath? To help or to harm?"

LUKE 6:9

How to live and how to pray

Matthew 5–7; Mark 3; Luke 6

✳

Jesus' reputation as a preacher continued to grow. His teaching gave new insights into the old laws and traditions.

From among his disciples, Jesus chose twelve to be apostles: Simon (whom he named Peter) and his brother Andrew; James and John, Philip and Bartholomew, Matthew and Thomas, James son of Alphaeus, and Simon (who was called the Patriot), Judas son of James, and Judas Iscariot, who became the traitor.

Luke 6:13–16

The number of Jesus' followers grew rapidly. From among them, Jesus chose twelve disciples whom he trusted to spread his message: the good news of how people could live as friends of God.

"Happy are those who know they have neglected the things of the spirit," he said. "The kingdom of heaven belongs to them.

"Happy are those who long to live as God wants: God will enable them to do so.

"Happy are those who work for peace: God will call them his children.

"Happy are those who stay loyal to God, even when they are cruelly treated for it. They will have their reward in heaven.

"Those who belong to God's kingdom are like light for the world. If you light a lamp in a dark room, you do not cover it with a bowl; you set it on a lamp stand so that everyone can see what they are doing. In the same way, my followers must let the light of their deeds shine before people. They will see the good things that you do and praise your Father God.

"Do not think that I have come to do away with the Law of Moses and teachings of the prophets. I am calling you all to be even more faithful to God.

"The Law sets a limit on the revenge a person can take. I am telling you not to seek revenge. If someone strikes you on one cheek, let them strike the other.

"If one of the occupation troops forces you to carry their pack for one mile, offer to carry it for two. When someone asks you for something, give it to them; be willing to lend to those who want to borrow.

"The traditional wisdom is to love your friends and hate your enemies. That's scarcely a virtue! I am telling you to love your enemies and pray for those who treat you badly. You must be as perfect in this as God, who allows the rain from heaven to fall on good people and bad people alike.

"Do not make a big show of your good deeds. God will see what you do and reward you. ✦

Jesus said, "You must be perfect — just as your Father in heaven is perfect!"

MATTHEW 5:48

217

"Do not stand up to pray in public places where you will be admired. Instead, go to your room, close the door, and say this simple prayer:

"Our Father in heaven:
may your holy name be honoured;
may your kingdom come;
may your will be done on earth as it is in heaven.
Give us today the food we need.
Forgive us the wrongs we have done,
as we forgive the wrongs that others have done to us.
Do not bring us to hard testing,
but keep us safe from the Evil One.

"Do not devote your lives to getting rich. Moths and rust will destroy even the most expensive possessions. Set your heart on doing the things that will make you rich in heaven.

"There is no compromise on this matter. You can't serve two masters. You must choose whether to serve God or money.

"Look at the wild birds. They don't sow crops, they don't toil over a harvest… and yet God provides food for them.

"And why worry about clothes? The wild flowers wear petals that are more beautiful than anything that King Solomon himself could afford.

"As God takes such care of the birds and flowers, you can be sure God will take care of you. ✌

"The gate to hell is wide and the road that leads there is easy. Many people travel it without thinking. The gate to life is narrow and the difficult path to it is one that few find.

"Listen to all I have said. If you obey my teaching, you are like the wise person who thinks carefully about where to build his house. He chooses the rock high above the flood. When the wind blows and the rain falls, his house is safe.

"If you listen to my teaching but then forget all its lessons, you are like the foolish person. He builds his house on the sand by the river. When the rain pours and the rivers flood and the wind howls around the eaves, the house collapses. Everything he has put his trust in comes crashing down." ✳

THE PURPOSE OF PARABLES

MATTHEW 13; MARK 4; LUKE 8, 13

✳

OFTEN, WHEN HE WAS PREACHING, JESUS TOLD PARABLES:
SIMPLE STORIES WITH A DEEPER MEANING ABOUT GOD'S
HEAVENLY KINGDOM.

One day, Jesus went down to the lakeside to
preach. A crowd quickly gathered, pressing
closer to hear what he had to say. More and more
people thronged close. In the end, Jesus had no
choice but to get in a boat that drifted in the
eddying shallows. From there, he continued to
speak and to tell many parables.

"There was once a man," he said, "who went out
to sow grain. He scattered handfuls from his
basket as he walked up and down the field.

"Some of the seed fell on the trampled path.
Birds swooped down and ate it up.

"Some fell on rocky ground. It soon sprouted,
but the soil was too shallow for the young
roots. As soon as the sun turned hot, the plants
withered.

"Some fell among thorn bushes. The seedlings
reached pale leaves up to the light, but were
choked by the stronger plants.

"But some of the seed fell in good, well-prepared

soil. The plants grew tall, flowered, and produced fine fat ears of grain… some of a hundred grains, some of sixty, others thirty."

Jesus' disciples exchanged glances. If they were puzzled by the story, what would the other listeners in the crowd make of it?

Once they were alone, they demanded to know. "Why do you speak in parables?" they clamoured. "We find them baffling."

"You have been chosen," replied Jesus, "to be the ones who do understand. ✍

Jesus concluded his parable with these words: "Listen, then, if you have ears!"

MATTHEW 13:9

223

Jesus said,
"I will use
parables when
I speak to
them; I will
tell them things
unknown since
the creation of
the world."

MATTHEW
13:35

"Listen: there are some people who hear what I say about the kingdom of heaven but do not understand. They are like the seeds on the path. The Evil One comes and snatches away the meaning.

"The seeds that fall on rocky ground are the people who hear the message and are instantly full of enthusiasm for it. However, they have not thought deeply about what it means to be my followers. As soon as they encounter problems, they give up.

"The seeds that fall among thorns are like those who hear my message and are attracted by it. But other things prove more attractive: home, work – getting rich. They don't put the message into practice.

"The seeds that fall on good soil are the people who hear my message and understand that they should make it their life's commitment. Their lives bear rich fruit, each according to their gifts.

"Here's another parable," Jesus said. "The kingdom of heaven is like a tiny seed. It grows into a tree with wide-spreading branches where all kinds of birds can come and make their nests. ✍

"The kingdom of heaven is also like yeast. A woman takes a handful of yeast and mixes it into a great bowlful of flour. She kneads the dough and leaves it. The tiny amount of yeast is enough to make the whole dough rise.

"Think of the kingdom of heaven like this. A man happens upon a hoard of treasure hidden in a field. He recognizes the enormous value of the find. Quietly, he covers it up again and then goes and sells everything he has in order to buy the field.

"Then again, imagine the kingdom of heaven like this. A merchant travels the world looking for fine pearls. He comes across one that is utterly perfect. Eagerly he goes and sells all his other treasures in order to have that one perfect thing.

"Some of you are fishermen," said Jesus. "I called you to come and help me fish for people.

"Think of the kingdom of heaven like this. The men take their boats out onto the lake and cast their nets. When they are full, they haul them in and sail back to shore. Then they settle down to divide the catch. The good fish go into buckets; the worthless ones are thrown away.

"At the end of time, the angels will come and sort good people from bad ones: the ones who belong in the kingdom and the others, who will face the consequences of a misspent life." ✳

WHO RULES THE STORM?

Matthew 8; Mark 4–5; Luke 8

✳

JESUS' MIRACLES SHOWED IN DIFFERENT WAYS THAT HE HAD
POWER OVER THE FORCES OF DEATH AND DESTRUCTION.

O ne day, when Jesus had finished preaching,
he returned to Capernaum. It was no
surprise to see a Roman officer in the streets
there: Roman troops occupied and policed the
entire country, and this particular officer had
made his home in the lakeside town.

What was surprising was the manner in
which he sped down the street.

"Sir," he cried desperately to Jesus, "I need
your help urgently."

Jesus' disciples stepped back nervously.
Roman soldiers could demand that locals
fetch and carry for them at will. Whatever
the Roman officer wanted was bound to be
inconvenient.

"Please," insisted the officer. "My servant
is sick in bed. He is in dreadful pain."

"Then I'll come and make him well,"
replied Jesus.

"Oh no, sir," replied the officer. "I don't
deserve to have you come to my house. It
will be enough for you to give the order for

my servant to be well again."

"Do you really think that?" asked Jesus in a surprised voice.

"Of course," said the soldier. "When my superior officers give me orders, I obey. When I give orders to my men, I expect them to obey at once."

Jesus turned to the people who were following him.

"I haven't seen faith like this among my own people," he said. "I assure you that the blessings God promised the people of Israel will be shared with people from every corner of the world."

He turned back to the officer. "Go home. You will find your servant well."

Later, as the sunset faded, Jesus and his disciples went down to the shore and got into a boat. It was their plan to sail to the other side of the lake in the dark hours.

The fishermen hoisted the sail and a steady breeze blew the boat along. Jesus fell asleep.

For an hour or more, all was well. Then, almost without warning, a storm hit. A fierce wind whipped up the waves and ripped at the sail.

"Everyone, get busy!" roared Simon. "You – help me get this canvas down... and the rest, get bailing."

The disciple nearest Jesus elbowed him awake. "Come on and do your bit," he shouted. "We'll die if we don't all work at bailing the water out." ✍

Jesus said to the officer, "What you believe will be done for you."

MATTHEW 8:13

Jesus shook himself awake and gazed at the turmoil. "Why are you frightened?" he said. "Have you no faith?"

He stood up. "Listen to me, wind," he said. "Be quiet.

"And you waves, just calm down."

All at once, the lake was calm; the wind no more than a gentle whisper.

Jesus wrapped his cloak around him as a blanket and lay down again. The disciples eyed him fearfully.

"What do think of that?" they whispered when they were sure he was asleep.

"Who can he be that he does such extraordinary things?"

The boat carried Jesus and his disciples safely to the region of Gerasa. They found a place to land away from the rocky cliffs into which burial caves had been cut.

As Jesus stepped ashore, a man came running down from the caves, shouting abuse and screaming nonsense. He flung himself at Jesus' feet.

"What have you come here for? What do you want with me? I know you're the Son of God... aren't you? Admit it!"

Jesus spoke quietly. "May the forces of evil leave you alone," he said.

"No, please – don't punish us!" the man screamed.

"Who are you?" asked Jesus, sharply. "Tell me your name."

"I'm Mob," snivelled the man. "I'm a crowd of demons in one worn-out body. A legion, an army... Be merciful, be kind... please."

"Leave the man alone," said Jesus.

"We will," came the answer. "But give us somewhere to go. Look at those pigs. We can go and be pigs, can't we?"

"Go, then," said Jesus.

The man's shriek echoed around the cliffs. The men looking after the pigs stopped their work to discover the cause of the commotion. As they watched, some strange panic took hold of the pigs. Squealing and grunting, they dashed headlong across the hillside and tumbled over the cliff into the lake.

In a panic, the swineherds ran off. Their story spread, and soon many local people gathered by the shore to find out what was going on.

They found Jesus and his disciples talking and laughing with the man who had for so long been rejected by his community. He seemed normal: someone had found him clothes to wear and his usual grimace had been replaced by a cheerful grin.

A spokesperson stepped forward. "I don't know what brought you here, Jesus," he said, "but I think you've caused enough trouble for one day. Please go away."

"Well," said Jesus to the man he had healed, "the best thing for you is to stay here. You can tell everyone what my message is all about."

With that, Jesus and his disciples set sail. ✳

Jesus said to the man, "Go back home and tell what God has done for you."

LUKE 8:39

233

JESUS AND THE WOMEN

MATTHEW 9; MARK 5; LUKE 8

✳

IN JESUS' DAY, MATTERS OF RELIGION WERE GENERALLY DEALT
WITH BY MEN. JESUS WAS DIFFERENT IN GIVING TIME AND
RESPECT TO WOMEN.

As Jesus went from place to place preaching, his twelve disciples went with him.

These men were not his only close followers. There were also women whom Jesus had healed who were devoted to helping him in his work. One of them was Mary, from the village of Magdala. Until she met Jesus, she had been shunned as mentally unstable, if not worse. Another follower was Joanna, whose husband held a very respectable post in local government. All of the women used their own money to help fund Jesus' work.

On the day that Jesus returned from Gerasa, another woman was waiting nervously to talk to him. She had been unwell for twelve years, and none of the doctors she had been to had been able to help her.

"Women of your age have to put up with these kinds of problems" was the kind of answer they gave.

Today, she hoped, would be different. Today she would not let herself be dismissed as beyond help.

Today she would ask Jesus to cure her.

First of all, she had to get near him. It became clear that was going to be difficult. A jostling crowd had gathered on the shore by the jetty. She could see one of the officials of the local synagogue trying to push his way to the front, and even he was being elbowed back and grumbled at.

"Poor Jairus," said a woman beside her. "I know why he's so eager to talk to Jesus. His little girl is awfully unwell. The other funeral singers and I are expecting the call to go to his house any moment."

The woman who was unwell bit her lip. Who would want to spare her a minute when Jairus' pretty young daughter was in such need? She watched Jairus pleading with Jesus, and the preacher nodding and asking a couple of his disciples to clear a path through the crowd. ✍

But they were coming her way. They were quite
near. If she didn't allow herself to be pushed aside,
if she just squeezed forward a bit… She'd done
it. She'd just managed to touch the edge of Jesus'
cloak as he went past. And she was better. Already,
she knew she was well again.

Jesus had stopped, barely out of reach.

"Who touched me?" he was saying, as he looked
around.

Those in the crowd who were closest were
shaking their heads. "Not me," they all protested.

"Don't worry about it," said Simon. "With all
these people milling about, it could have been

anyone. I'm sure whoever touched you didn't do it deliberately."

"They did," said Jesus. "I felt power go out of me." He gazed questioningly at the faces around him.

The woman who had been healed felt deeply embarrassed. Even so, she knew it was right to speak up. "It was me," she said, and she knelt down to show her respect. "I can explain," she said hesitantly. As she began to speak, her whole story tumbled out.

"I understand," said Jesus. "But you can be happy now. You are cured."

Even as Jesus was speaking, a messenger arrived. "It's bad news," he whispered to Jairus. "I'm very sorry: your daughter has just died."

Jairus' face twisted with sorrow, but Jesus swept him along. "I'm still coming to see her," he said. "Don't be afraid."

When he reached the house, a cluster of women had already arrived. They were wailing and weeping in the customary display of shared grief.

"You don't need to do that," Jesus told them. "The girl is only sleeping."

The mourners' song trailed away. "What do you know?" snapped one. "We know how unwell the child has been. We've seen the corpse; that lovely, innocent face – she was only twelve. How dare you raise the father's hopes with easy lies!" ໔

Jesus said to the woman, "Go in peace: your faith has made you well."

LUKE 8:48

Jesus said to Jairus, "Only believe and your daughter will be well."

LUKE 8:50

Jesus remained unflustered. He asked three of his disciples – Simon, John, and James – to help him show the mourners out of the house. Then they went into the room where Jairus' daughter lay.

Jesus took her by the hand. "Come on, little girl," he said. "Time to get up."

The little girl shifted and sighed. Then she sat up. "Oh," she said. "What's happening? Did I oversleep?"

Jairus and his wife rushed forward to hug their daughter.

"There," said Jesus. "Don't go around creating a stir about what happened. Just make your daughter a good meal and take good care of her." ✳

THE BREAD OF LIFE

JOHN 6

✳

JESUS ONCE WORKED A MIRACLE TO FEED A CROWD OF FIVE THOUSAND. THE GOSPEL OF JOHN EXPLAINS THAT THE EVENT POINTED TO A DEEPER TRUTH ABOUT JESUS.

One day, Jesus and his disciples sailed to the remoter side of Lake Galilee. They tied the boat up, climbed a hill, and sat on the grass, enjoying the peaceful scene below.

Then, to their astonishment, they saw a crowd of people hurrying along the shore. By the time the great mass of people reached the boat, they could hear the hubbub of chatter, peals of laughter, and excitable shouts.

"Up there! I can see them!" cried someone. Almost at once, the crowd turned to look where he was pointing; then they began streaming up the hill.

Jesus turned to one of his disciples, Philip. "Where can we buy food to feed all these people?" he asked.

"Feed them!" exclaimed Philip. "What makes you think we could feed them? It would take – I don't know – more than half a year's wages. Perhaps… two hundred silver coins. But that wouldn't give anyone more than a mouthful. What's more, we don't have that kind of money."

Jesus spent the day preaching to the crowds and healing those who were sick. Everyone had made a huge effort to see Jesus and their attention never wavered. As the sun sank low, the disciples decided Jesus had been busy for long enough.

"It's not a good idea to keep the people out here any longer," they told him. "Send them off to the farms and villages nearby so they can get some food."

"I want you to give them something to eat," was the reply. It left the disciples baffled.

"We can't afford it," Philip reminded Jesus.

"This young lad has made a kind offer," said Andrew. "He heard what we were talking about and has said we can share his food: five loaves and two fish. It's very generous of him, but it won't be enough for all these people."

"Just ask the people to sit down," said Jesus, "in groups of about fifty." ❧

Jesus welcomed the crowds, spoke to them about the kingdom of God, and healed those who needed it.

Luke 9:11

They did so. As the crowd settled down, Jesus took the bread, said a prayer of thanks to God, and shared it out. He did the same with the fish.

Everyone took a portion of the food and passed it on. By a miracle, there was enough for everyone – about five thousand people. Everyone had as much as they wanted. ✑

People in the crowd whispered among themselves, "Surely this is the Prophet who was to come into the world!"

JOHN 6:14

When the meal was over, Jesus spoke to his disciples. "I want you to gather up the leftover pieces. It's not right to waste food."

The disciples set to work, and together they filled twelve baskets of scraps.

People from the crowd watched closely as the miracle unfolded in front of them.

"This Jesus must surely be from God – he must be the one who will lead our people into a whole new era of freedom."

"We must do all we can to make sure the opportunity doesn't pass by."

"Let's make him king. Bring on the revolution!"

Jesus quickly became aware of what they were planning. Before they had time to act, he slipped away into the hills by himself. "I need to spend some time praying," he whispered to his disciples. "Don't wait here for me."

When evening fell, the disciples got back into the boat and set off toward Capernaum. As the sky grew darker, the wind got up, and the water grew choppy. The disciples rowed hard to make headway, blinking as the cold spray stung their faces and numbed their hands.

Suddenly, one of them gave a cry. "Look at that whirl of spray… It looks as if there's a ghost out there."

As the pale figure approached, the twelve men crouched lower in the boat, terrified.

"Don't be afraid," said the vision. "It's me! Can't you tell?"

Jesus gave a broad smile as he took hold of the gunwale, and his friends eagerly hauled him aboard.

"That gave us a fright," they agreed, trying to sound as if everything was normal. Only when they thought he was no longer listening did they whisper that Jesus must surely have power from God to do the things he did.

As the new day dawned, the people whom Jesus had fed were astonished to find him back in Capernaum. "When did you get here?" they wanted to know.

"You have come looking because of the food I gave," he told them. "Sadly, you don't understand the meaning of the miracle.

"Don't spend your lives working for ordinary food, which perishes so quickly. Instead, work for the food that lasts for eternal life.

"What God wants you to do is to believe in the one he sent." ✳

Jesus said, "I am the bread of life. Those who come to me will never be hungry; those who believe in me will never be thirsty."

JOHN 6:35

Jesus and the Children

✳

Jesus had called his disciples to help him spread the news of the kingdom of God. However, he warned them, they were not to grow proud.

Sometimes – especially when they thought Jesus was not listening – the disciples argued. They all knew that Jesus was their leader, but which of them was the most important after that?

"I think it's me," Simon Peter would say. "He nicknamed me Peter – the Rock – because he knows my loyalty is unshakeable. He can rely on me to help build up his following."

"I think it's John," said another. "He and Jesus have the longest conversations. I think he'd trust John with anything – even his mother's life."

"Well," said James, who was John's brother. "It's hard to say, but Simon Peter and Andrew, John and me – we were the ones he chose first."

One day, after a particularly heated argument, the disciples decided there was only one way to settle the quarrel. They went to Jesus.

"Tell us," they said, "who is the greatest in the kingdom of heaven?"

Jesus looked at them sternly. He could guess what they'd been talking about. Then he called to a child who was watching them. "Come over here. Just come and stand near me, so my disciples can all see you."

The child smiled with delight. Mostly, children were told not to bother grown-ups.

"Now listen," said Jesus to his disciples. "You have got to change the way you think about everything. Unless you become like children, you will never be part of the kingdom.

"The greatest person in God's kingdom is the one who acts humbly and accepts my teaching as openly and honestly as children do.

"What is more, you are to welcome children. When you do that, it is as if you are welcoming me.

"Take care not to discourage children or make them lose faith in my teaching. Remember, God has put each of them in the charge of an angel. ❧

Jesus said, "See that you don't despise any of these little ones. Their angels in heaven are always in the presence of my Father in heaven."

MATTHEW
18:10

"Think of shepherds, and how they take care of their flocks. A man might have one hundred sheep. Even though he has so many, every one of them is precious.

"What would such a man do if, when it came to counting his flock, he found that there were only ninety-nine? Would he shrug as if it didn't matter?

"Of course not. He would leave the ninety-nine grazing safely on the hillside and then he would go looking. He might have to walk miles to find a lost sheep. He might have to tramp along steep and stony paths and pick his way through thorns and brambles. You can be sure he would never give up until he had found his missing animal.

"Then, when he had found it, would he beat the creature for causing him trouble? Of course not. He would simply be happy to have a complete flock again. He would pick that sheep up with strong arms and gently carry it home.

"Then, when the sheep was safely in the fold, he would call his friends to come and celebrate with him.

"God is rather like that shepherd: God does not want even little ones to be lost. When anyone who was lost is found, all heaven rejoices." ∾

Jesus' disciples heard all these things... but they did not really take them to heart. It was not very long after that some mothers came to Jesus, bringing their children with them.

They spoke first to the disciples. They had no choice about that – the men had made it their job to stop time-wasters bothering their master.

"Please," said the women, "we'd just like Jesus to say a prayer for these little ones. Nothing complicated, you understand; we'd just like him to ask God to bless them."

"Sorry," said the disciples. "That's really not a priority for him. He's got important people eager to come and discuss weighty matters of religion;

he's got people who are seriously in need of help. It was really rather foolish to think he'd have time for your brood; after all – what would they understand of what he has to say?"

Jesus' voice rang out. "Bring the children here," he said. "Don't try to stop them. Remember what I said: the kingdom of heaven belongs to such as these." ✳

THE GOOD SAMARITAN

LUKE 10

✳

LONG BEFORE THE TIME OF JESUS, THE NORTHERN KINGDOM
OF ISRAEL HAD BEEN DEFEATED IN WAR. THE VICTORS FORCED
ITS PEOPLE TO LIVE IN ANOTHER LAND, AND ANOTHER DEFEATED
PEOPLE WERE MADE TO LIVE IN THE OLD KINGDOM, WHICH
BECAME KNOWN AS SAMARIA. THE JEWS OF JESUS' DAY
DETESTED THE SAMARITANS.

*"Israel,
remember this!
The Lord —
and the Lord
alone — is our
God. Love the
Lord your God
with all your
heart, with all
your soul, and
with all your
strength."*

DEUTERONOMY
6:4–5

The teachers of the Jewish law were suspicious of Jesus. They knew that his teaching and his miracles drew the crowds… but was he misleading the people? One day, a teacher of the Law decided to ask Jesus a sly question — one that would show up the flaws in his preaching.

"Teacher," he said flatteringly. "Please help me with a really fundamental question: what must I do to have eternal life?"

Jesus looked at the man. He could tell that he was not really seeking advice. "You know the Scriptures," said Jesus. "What do they say?"

"All of the Law is summed up in two commandments," said the man. "'Love the Lord your God with all your heart, with all your soul, with all your strength, and with all your mind.'

"The second follows on naturally from that:

'Love your neighbour as you love yourself.'"

"You are right," said Jesus. "Do those things and you will live."

The teacher frowned. Had his question been so quickly dismissed?

"The real puzzle," protested the man, "is this: who is my neighbour?"

"Here's a story," said Jesus. "There was once a man who decided to go from Jerusalem to Jericho. In the lonely road that winds down through the hills, robbers attacked him. They beat him up, stole all his belongings, and left him for dead.

"It so happened that a priest from the Temple was passing that way. He saw the man lying in the road but wanted nothing to do with it, and he simply passed by on the other side.

"Next came a Levite – one of the helpers in the Temple. He crept up to take a closer look at the wounded body, shuddered, and hurried on. ✍

"Do not take revenge on anyone or continue to hate him, but love your neighbour as you love yourself. I am the Lord."

LEVITICUS 19:18

"Then came a Samaritan. He saw the man and knew in his heart that he wanted to help in any way he could.

"He went over and lifted him up. He cleaned the wounds and bandaged them. Then gently he helped the man onto his own donkey and took him to an inn. 🙒

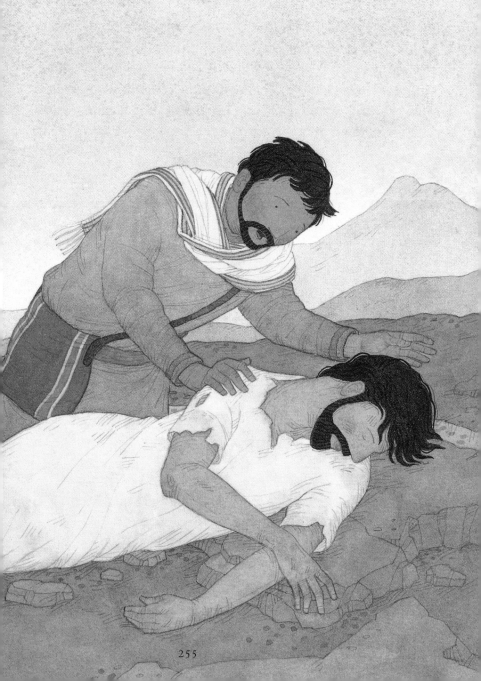

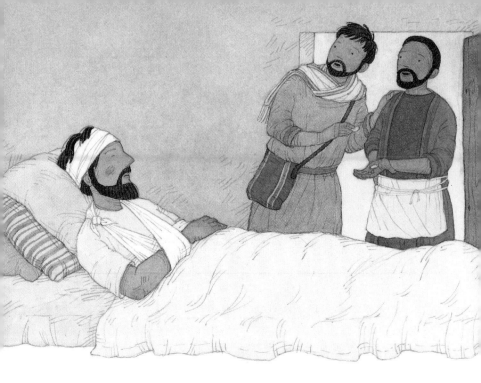

"Any plans the Samaritan had for how to spend the evening he abandoned without hesitation. He spent all his time taking care of the man and making sure he could sleep comfortably.

"The next day, he had to travel on. Before he left, he took out a considerable sum — two silver coins — and gave them to the innkeeper.

" 'The poor man I brought here yesterday will need to spend some time getting better,' he explained. 'This money is to pay you to take care of him. If it costs you any more, just make a note of what you spend. I will pay you back when I come this way again.' "

Jesus paused, and the teacher of the Law who

had come to question him frowned slightly. He could tell what the story was pointing at. Jesus had deliberately told it to show two religious leaders from the Jewish people failing to show even basic decency. By contrast, a Samaritan – a foreigner whose understanding of the God of Israel was at best superstitious – had carried out the obligations of the Law without any sense of pride or self-righteousness.

"So," said Jesus, "in your opinion, which of these three acted like a neighbour to the man who was attacked by robbers?"

"The one who was kind to him," came the grudging reply.

"You are right again," said Jesus. "You can go away from here with your questions answered... and ready to do the same as that man." ✳

Jesus said, "Do for others what you want them to do for you: this is the meaning of the Law of Moses and of the teachings of the prophets."

MATTHEW 7:12

THE FORGIVING FATHER

LUKE 15

✳

IN JESUS' DAY, THE RELIGIOUS LEADERS KEPT THEIR DISTANCE
FROM THOSE WHO DID NOT LEAD RESPECTABLE LIVES.
HOW COULD JESUS BE A SERIOUS TEACHER IF HE DID NOT
DO THE SAME?

Among the crowds who gathered to listen to
Jesus were all kinds and conditions of people.
Decent, honest, and respectable people sat side
by side with those they would normally shun.
Some were beggars or poor wretches who found
themselves excluded from everyday society because
of disfiguring ailments. Others were notorious
wrongdoers, such as the many tax collectors
who worked for the occupying Romans,
simply because it was a way to get rich.
The religious teachers disapproved
entirely. "Treating such people as his
friends is quite against the spirit of
our faith," they grumbled. "If Jesus
wants to be taken seriously as a
teacher, he should live a pure and
holy life."

Jesus told a parable to help his
doubters see the world as God
sees it.

"There was once a man who had two sons. The elder worked diligently on the family farm and helped make it prosperous. The younger dreamed of all the exciting things he could do if only he had the money.

"He began to pester his father. 'One day, I'll inherit a share of this farm,' he said. 'But who knows when that will be? I'll probably be too old to enjoy it.

" 'Why not give me my inheritance now? I'm young and ambitious. I want to go to the city and make something really special of my life.'

"The father sighed. There was a good deal of risk in what his son was proposing... but he loved the boy and wanted to give him a chance. So he transferred part of the land he owned into his son's name, and watched with some anxiety as the young man sold it and left home with plenty of money.

"He went to a big city far away. The temptations to spend were everywhere. Not that he was bothered; he had plenty of money for luxury living, and he enjoyed every moment. He spent and spent as if his fortune were limitless. ✎

Jesus said, "There will be more joy in heaven over one sinner who repents than over ninety-nine respectable people who do not need to repent."

LUKE 15:7

"However, city dwellers depend on good harvests as much as farming people do. When the crops failed, famine struck. The price of everything rose rapidly. The young man found himself out of money, unable to pay for a place to stay or a crust to eat.

"In desperation, he went looking for work. The only experience he had was on the farm, and a local landowner agreed to hire him to look after a herd of pigs.

"It was soul-destroying work. The animals grunted contentedly among themselves as they rolled in the dust, only to come squealing impatiently when the young man brought the buckets of food.

"He scattered the bean pods to stop them knocking him over in their impatience and watched jealously as they scoffed and snuffled.

" 'I could eat that stuff myself, I'm so hungry,' he grumbled aloud. 'I was expecting to have at least one meal a day provided.'

"Although he was desperate for food, the pods proved tough and bitter. He spat out the chewed fibres and wept with misery.

" 'My father gives his servants more than they can eat, and here am I about to starve.' As he railed against his misfortune, an idea came to him.

" 'I shall give up this wretched job and go back home. I'll say to my father, "I've done the wrong thing: wrong by your standards and wrong by God's standards. I don't deserve to be called your son, but I would be grateful to be taken on as a servant."'

"With that, he started out, trudging the long miles in worn-out sandals.

"He barely looked up when he crested the hill from which he could first make out the cluster of buildings that he had once called home. But on a flat roof there, his father was sitting in the shade of a fig tree, watching the road and remembering the day he had watched his son walk out of his life.

"Then he saw the lonely figure coming nearer… and he recognized him. He almost tumbled down in his haste and ran along the road to greet his son, arms wide in welcome. ❧

"As he hugged his boy tight, he heard the words of heartfelt apology.

" 'Don't worry about that,' he laughed. 'You're home! That's all that matters.'

"He called out to the servants as they entered the house. 'Look who's back! Tonight we must have a feast – we'll roast a whole calf – and share our good news.

" 'Go and get this ragamuffin properly dressed so he looks like what he is: the son I'm proud of, the guest of honour.'

"Meanwhile, the elder son was making his way home from the fields. He was surprised to hear music and dancing, and asked a servant to explain.

" 'It's your brother,' came the reply. 'Your father is celebrating his return.'

"At that, the elder brother flew into a rage. He was so angry that he would not even go into the house. His father came out and begged him to join the party.

" 'Why should I?' his son shouted. 'I've been loyal all these years, and you never even let me have my friends around for a decent meal. My younger brother squanders a fortune, and you treat him like this.'

" 'My son,' said the father. 'Everything I have is yours. But we had to celebrate your brother's return. It is as if he were back from the dead.' " ✳

The young man said, "Father, I have sinned against God and against you. I am no longer fit to be called your son."

Luke 15:21

The father said, "We had to celebrate and be happy, because your brother was lost, but now he has been found."

Luke 15:32

JESUS AND THE TAX COLLECTOR

LUKE 11, 18–19

✳

THE PHARISEES THOUGHT IT RIGHT TO AVOID ANY CONTACT
WITH WRONGDOERS. TO THEIR DISMAY, JESUS MINGLED WITH
ALL KINDS OF PEOPLE AND EVEN ATE WITH THEM.

One day when Jesus had been preaching, a
Pharisee invited him to dinner. The Pharisee
ran his household strictly, being careful to observe
every last detail of the religious law, and almost at
once, the way Jesus was acting upset him.

"Excuse me," he fussed, "but I see that you have
taken your place without washing your hands. I'm
sure you know how we Pharisees understand the
Law on such matters. I'm rather surprised that you
are not more scrupulous. After all, you do claim to
be a teacher."

His voice trailed off once he realized that
Jesus did not look in the least
perturbed.

"The truth is,"
replied Jesus, "that
you Pharisees are
paying attention to
the wrong things.

264

You fuss and fret about the rituals of washing hands and cups and plates as if that were the way to live pure and holy lives. Inside, you let anger get the better of you and plot all kinds of evil deeds. Share your food and drink with the poor, and then your cups and plates will really be clean.

"You Pharisees have worked out how to observe the Law about giving God a tenth of your wealth down to the tiniest detail. You even tithe kitchen herbs and count out the leaves of mint and rue that you owe to God. You are so busy with these tiny matters that you forget to ensure that the poor get justice.

"You love it when people look up to you in the synagogues and admire you for your learning and your long prayers. You preach about all the laws they must keep if they are to please God, but with so much detail that you make life a misery."

The Pharisee was dismayed by Jesus' directness, and he could hardly wait for an opportunity to complain to his friends.

"Jesus may be original in what he says, but his teaching is so very wrong," they agreed. "He doesn't care about the Law, and everything he says is designed to give the impression that God doesn't care about standards. We have to stop him! We have to stand up for what we believe in!" ❧

Jesus said, "Do not think that I have come to do away with the Law of Moses and the teachings of the prophets. I have not come to do away with them, but to make their teachings come true."

MATTHEW 5:17

*The tax
collector said
this prayer:
"God, have
pity on me, a
sinner!"*

LUKE 18:13

One day, Jesus told a parable to show what God
thinks about those who are sure of their own
goodness and who look down on others.

"Once," he said, "two men went to the Temple to
pray. One was a Pharisee; the other, a tax collector.

"The Pharisee stood a little apart from everyone
else to say his prayer. 'I thank you, God,' he began,
'that your Law enables me to live righteously.
Those who neglect your Law fall into so many
vices: they are greedy and dishonest; they are not
faithful in marriage. There is a tax collector here
whose life is ruined by such wrongdoing.

"'As for me, it is a privilege to serve you. I fast
two days every week. I give you a tenth of all my
income. My life is dedicated to your Law.'"

266

"Then the Pharisee turned and bustled out of the Temple, his head held high.

"The tax collector simply hung his head.

"'God have mercy on me,' he said. 'I have done so many wrong things I can't even begin to name them.'

"Let me tell you," explained Jesus, "it was the tax collector who went home at peace with God, and not the Pharisee. For those who think they are wonderful will be humbled, but those who acknowledge their failings will be forgiven and made welcome in the kingdom."

Some time after, Jesus started out for Jerusalem. His journey took him through Jericho, where crowds came out to see him.

It so happened that the chief tax collector there was a very short man. Zacchaeus had made himself rich by demanding a lot more money from the people than he needed to pass on to his Roman masters, and everyone hated him for it. When people saw that he was trying to squeeze his way through to the front of the crowd, they cheerfully elbowed him back.

Then Zacchaeus had an idea. He could climb a tree. Years had passed since he'd last done so… but there was a sycamore fig with conveniently placed branches from which he would get a good view. ❧

Jesus said, "All those who make themselves great will be humbled, and all who humble themselves will be made great."

LUKE 18:14

267

So he did. And Jesus came right to the foot of the tree. Then, to Zacchaeus's astonishment, he looked up.

"Come down, Zacchaeus!" said Jesus. "I want to stay at your house today."

Zacchaeus's descent was not elegant. For one thing, he was trying to hurry, and for another, the crowd was jeering, which made him clumsy.

The townsfolk were grumbling about Jesus too. "It's hard to believe that preacher is a good judge of character," they said. "That tax man's a crook."

Meanwhile, Zacchaeus led the way home. He ordered his servants to prepare a dinner worthy of their very important guest. All through the meal, he listened eagerly to everything Jesus had to say. What he heard was an inspiration.

He stood up and made an announcement in front of his household and all the guests. "Listen. I have made a decision. I am going to give half of what I own to the poor. If I have cheated anyone – and I am aware that may be the case – I will pay back four times as much."

Jesus stood up to give his reply. "Today," he said, "someone has been saved from the slippery slope of wrongdoing. Zacchaeus really is a descendant of Abraham – one of God's people. I have come to look for those who have made the wrong choices in life and to rescue them." ✳

Jesus said, "The Son of Man came to seek and to save the lost."

LUKE 19:10

The First Christians

When Jesus was alive, he had many followers. However, the term "Christians" only came into being after his death.

Those who followed Jesus during his lifetime did so for a variety of reasons. Some were truly eager to listen to his preaching and take it to heart. Others simply wanted to be entertained and hoped to see a miracle. There were still others who wanted to believe that Jesus was going to challenge the Romans and make himself king.

Indeed, when Jesus rode into Jerusalem for the Passover festival one year, the crowds shouted, "God bless the king who comes in the name of the Lord!" They were hoping that Jesus' arrival marked the start of a rebellion. Even though Jesus' enemies tried to persuade the Roman governor in Jerusalem, Pontius Pilate, that Jesus was a dangerous rebel, it was clear there was no evidence to support the accusation. The kingdom that Jesus preached about would not be ushered in through violence.

Nevertheless, Pilate did agree to Jesus' execution – to avoid a clash with the religious leaders and the noisy crowd they assembled. At this point, those who admired Jesus for his miracles hoped that he might be able to use his powers to save himself. They were dismayed at the way he humbly submitted to crucifixion.

Even Jesus' most devoted followers, who believed that his preaching was good and true, were devastated by his death. They thought that everything Jesus had preached about was over. They were astonished at the first reports that some women had seen Jesus alive again. Then Jesus appeared among them.

The resurrection, they said, was the greatest miracle of all. It was clear proof that Jesus was indeed God's chosen king: the messiah, the Christ. Those who wanted to be his followers needed to turn away from wrongdoing and accept the forgiveness of which Jesus had preached. The sign of their decision was to be baptized "in the name of Jesus Christ".

Many did so. It was the belief among them that Jesus was not merely a good and wise man but also the Christ that soon earned them the name of Christians.

Eagerly these first Christians began to spread the message throughout the Roman empire.

Jesus in Jerusalem

MATTHEW 21, 23; MARK 11–12; LUKE 19–21

✳

THE RELIGIOUS LEADERS WERE VEXED BY JESUS AND HIS
TEACHING. WHEN HE CAME TO JERUSALEM TO CELEBRATE THE
PASSOVER, THEY WERE IN THE MOOD FOR A SHOWDOWN.

Jesus was on his way to Jerusalem for the
Passover. As he and his disciples came near the
city, he sent two of them ahead with instructions:
"I want you to hurry on to the next village. There,
you will find a donkey tethered. It is only a colt
and has never been ridden. I want you to untie it
and bring it here. If anyone challenges you, simply
say, 'The Master needs it.'"

Everything turned out just as Jesus had said. The
disciples brought the donkey to Jesus and threw
their cloaks over it to make a seat. As Jesus started
out, people spread their cloaks on the road in front
of him as if for a great parade.

He soon came to place where the road goes down
from the Mount of Olives before rising again to
Jerusalem. The crowd had grown larger and livelier.
Some cut palm branches to carpet the ground in
front of Jesus. Others waved branches and chanted,
"God bless the king who comes in the name of the
Lord! Alleluia!" ✍

There were some Pharisees in the crowd who were enraged by what they heard.

They marched up to Jesus. "Teacher," they said, "you must tell your followers to be quiet. All this talk of your being God's chosen king is dangerous nonsense."

"You can be sure," replied Jesus, "that if I tell my followers to be quiet, the stones themselves will start shouting."

He rode on to the city and went to the Temple. In its outer courtyard, the festival market was a riot of noise. Passover pilgrims were haggling with traders to exchange their money for Temple coins; others were arguing about the price of the animals to buy as sacrifices. Jesus' face clouded with anger. Then he marched over and overturned first one table... and then another, and another. Coins jingled to the ground and ran along the paving stones. Sheep and cattle escaped their pens and began to run, while doves fluttered from their cages.

"The Scriptures tell us that the Temple is to be a place of prayer," shouted Jesus. "You are making it a den of thieves. Get out! The lot of you!"

In the colonnades around the courtyard, the priests gathered with other religious leaders.

"We've given this Jesus plenty of warnings that his behaviour is unacceptable," they agreed. "We will have to get rid of him."

Jesus wept at the sight of the city and said, "O Jerusalem – if only you knew today what is needed for peace! But now you cannot see it!"

LUKE 19:41–42

Yet even the most influential of Jesus' enemies could not see an easy way to do so. They watched grimly as, day after day, Jesus returned to the Temple and preached to those who gathered to listen.

On one occasion the priests and religious teachers came and challenged him: "What right do you have to say the things you do?" they demanded to know.

"Let me ask you a question," replied Jesus. "John was well known for baptizing people as a sign of their turning back to God. Who gave him the right – God or human beings?"

The priests and teachers turned away haughtily and huddled in a far corner. "We can't say John had God's authority to baptize," they agreed, "because then Jesus will ask why we didn't respect what he did. But if we say that human beings gave him authority, the people will turn on us. Everyone thought he was a prophet." ✍

They returned to Jesus and declared, "We don't know where John got his authority from."

"Well then," said Jesus, "I won't tell you who gives me the right to be a preacher."

The priests and teachers went away feeling angry and defeated. Then they had another idea: they would bribe people to mingle with his eager followers and ask questions designed to get him into trouble with the Roman authorities. The spies were duly found and sent off to do their work.

"Teacher," they asked, "we know that you tell your followers to respect God alone, as the ancient Law demands. Tell us – is it lawful for us to pay taxes to the Roman emperor?"

Jesus saw the ruse. "Show me a silver coin," he said. "Whose face and name are on it?"

"The emperor's," came the reply.

"Then pay the emperor what belongs to him," said Jesus, "and pay God what belongs to God."

The spies had no response. They failed to catch him out with any of their other questions. Even so, it was clear to Jesus' followers that tensions were mounting.

"Beware of the teachers of the Law," Jesus told the crowds. "They love to walk about in their long robes and be treated with respect. They like to be given the best place in the synagogue and at feasts. They make a great show of saying their prayers. Yet they care nothing for justice. They demand that the poorest of widows pay their offerings even if it leaves them homeless."

Jesus turned to look at the row of boxes set out for people to make their gifts to the Temple treasury. Rich people sauntered up and dropped in their offerings. Some gave it little thought; others flung their coins and made an ostentatious clatter.

Behind them came a poor widow. She dropped in her offering of two copper coins.

"See that," exclaimed Jesus. "The other people we saw gave from what they had to spare. That widow has been forced to give all she had to live on." ✳

THE LAST SUPPER

LUKE 22; JOHN 13–14

✳

AT THE LAST SUPPER JESUS SHARED WITH HIS DISCIPLES,
HE SHOWED THEM WHAT THEY MUST DO WHEN HE WAS NO
LONGER WITH THEM.

It was nearly time for the Jews to celebrate the
Passover festival: the time to remember how,
long ago, God had worked miracles to allow the
people to escape from slavery in Egypt; the time to
recall the Law and the covenant – the great promise
that those who obeyed God's laws would be God's
people.

This year, however, the priests and the religious
leaders were consumed with another matter: how
to have Jesus put to death.

They were delighted when one of Jesus' own
disciples, Judas Iscariot, came to them in secret and
offered to betray him. For thirty pieces of silver, he
agreed to help them arrest Jesus when he was away
from the adoring crowds.

Jesus knew how events were unfolding.
Undeterred, he calmly asked Simon Peter and John
to prepare a special festival meal. In a borrowed
room on an upper floor, they set the table with the
traditional foods and plenty of wine.

In the evening, Jesus and his disciples all met

there. Suddenly, Jesus took off his outer garment and wrapped a towel around his waist. Then he poured some water into a basin. With this, he began to wash his disciples' feet clean of the dust of the day — a custom at the time and the job of a lowly servant.

Simon Peter was at first indignant that his master should humble himself in this way. However, when the task was complete, Jesus explained the reason.

"You call me Lord and Teacher, and that is indeed what I am," he said. "Yet tonight I have acted as your servant and washed your feet. From now on, you must do the same for one another."

Then he took his place at table again. At the meal, he took a piece of bread, gave thanks to God, broke it, and shared it with them. ✍

Jesus said, "I have set an example for you, so that you will do just what I have done for you."

John 13:15

"This is my body, which is given for you," he said. "Do this in memory of me."

After supper, he took the cup of wine and shared it with them. "This cup is God's new covenant sealed with my blood, which is poured out for you," he said.

"Indeed, one of you here is going to betray me and allow my enemies to kill me." ❧

The disciples may have been puzzled by what Jesus said about a new covenant, but they were dismayed by the announcement that one of their number was a traitor. Barely noticing as Judas left the room – presumably on some errand – they began to argue among themselves about who it could be.

Simon Peter insisted that he was the most loyal of any of them.

"If there's trouble," he said to Jesus, "I'll stay with you. I don't care if we get thrown into prison. I'm ready to die with you."

"Brave words," cautioned Jesus, "but before the cockerel crows at dawn, you will deny me three times.

Jesus said, "Now I give you a new commandment: love one another."

JOHN 13:34

"You cannot go where I am going," he continued, "but I leave you with a new commandment: love one another. As I have loved you, so you must love one another. That way, everyone will know that you are my disciples.

"There's no need to feel worried or upset about what lies ahead," continued Jesus. "Believe in God and believe in me. In my Father's house there are many rooms, and I am simply going ahead to prepare a place for you. Then I will come and take you there. Indeed, you know the way there already."

"How can we know?" protested Thomas. "You haven't actually told us where you're going, so we can't know how to get there."

Jesus replied, "I am the way, the truth, and the life; no one goes to the Father except by me.

"If you really want to be my followers, do the things I have told you to do. I will ask God the Father to send the Holy Spirit to help you and strengthen you.

"As for me, I will not be able to be with you and talk to you for much longer. A chain of events has begun, and through it God's plan will come true.

"We cannot even stay in this room much longer. Come: let us go the olive grove of Gethsemane, where we have been sleeping under the stars these last few days."

With that, Jesus and eleven disciples set off into the night. ✷

Jesus said, "Peace is what I leave with you; it is my own peace that I give you."

JOHN 14:27

BETRAYED AND CRUCIFIED

LUKE 22–23

✳

IN THE TIME OF THE ROMANS, COMMON CRIMINALS WHO
WERE GIVEN THE DEATH SENTENCE WERE NAILED TO A CROSS
OF WOOD: CRUCIFIED.

Jesus said to God, "Not my will, however, but your will be done."

LUKE 22:42

In the dark olive grove, Jesus whispered urgently to his disciples.

"Pray," he said, "and ask God to help you escape the trials that lie ahead."

He himself went a short way away from them and fell on his knees, shaking. "Father, if it is your will, please spare me from suffering," he prayed. "Surely, surely there is another way to achieve your purpose."

After a long time pleading with God, Jesus went back to his disciples. He found them asleep. "Get up!" he told them. You should be praying for God's help to get through this dreadful time."

He was still speaking when the shadowy figures surged around them. Judas hurried forward and kissed Jesus, as was the custom.

"So is that how you betray me?" asked Jesus sadly, looking beyond to the priests and members of the Temple guard Judas had brought with him.

"This is the time when the power of darkness rules," Jesus sighed.

The soldier hustled Jesus away to the house of the high priest. Simon Peter followed at a distance. He edged into the courtyard and sat by the fire there while servants bustled around. After a some time, a servant girl peered at him. "This man was with Jesus!" she exclaimed.

"You're wrong, you foolish woman," Simon Peter snapped. "I don't even know him."

The raised voices made the other servants more curious. They gathered in silent groups, watching. Then one man spoke up. "I recognize you. The woman is right. You're one of Jesus' followers."

"I certainly am not!" hissed Simon Peter. He huddled closer to the fire and gazed intently at the flames.

An hour passed. Then another man came up. "We've no doubt at all that you were with Jesus. Your Galilean accent gives you away."

"I tell you, I don't know what you are talking about!" cried Simon Peter.

At that moment, a cockerel crowed. Simon Peter remembered that Jesus had said he would deny knowing him three times before the night was over. He went outside and wept. ✍

Through the night, the guards who had arrested Jesus mocked him cruelly. It was not until daybreak that the summons came to bring him to the meeting room where the chief priests and religious leaders had gathered.

"Tell us," they demanded, "are you the messiah?"

"You won't believe me, whatever I say," replied Jesus. "And if I ask a question, you won't answer."

Back and forth they argued, determined to make Jesus say something that would incriminate him. Eventually, they asked, "Are you the Son of God?"

"You say I am," replied Jesus.

"That's it!" came the cry. "We don't need witnesses now. We have your own wicked claim about yourself... a claim that is an insult to God."

However, while they were certain that a religious crime had been committed, they had no authoriy to punish. Only the Roman governor, Pontius Pilate, could give the order for the death penalty. At once, the priests and leaders marched Jesus off to stand trial before him.

"This man is leading our people astray," they told him. "He's telling people not to pay taxes to the emperor. Instead, he claims that he is a king sent by God."

Their words were treacherous, chosen carefully to make

Jesus look like a rebel. Pilate, however, was wise enough to see that the young preacher had done nothing to threaten his authority.

"I see no reason to condemn this man," he declared. "However, as the governor of Galilee is here in the city, I am happy for him to question Jesus."

The governor, a man named Herod, was delighted to see Jesus. He had heard stories of his many miracles, and he was hoping that Jesus might entertain him with some wonderworking. Jesus, however, refused even to answer his questions. After a while, Herod realized the interview was getting no result, so he sent Jesus back to Pilate.

"You present me with a problem," Pilate told the priests. "I'm inclined to have Jesus whipped by way of a warning and then to let him go."

By now, however, a crowd had gathered. It was the custom for the people to ask the governor to release a prisoner at Passover time. They began baying for Pilate to release a notorious criminal named Barabbas.

Pilate went to speak to them. "I can release Jesus for you," he declared.

"Kill him! Crucify him!" came the cry. It turned to chanting: persistent, angry... dangerous. In the end, Pilate decided to let them have their way to avoid a riot. ❧

The soldiers who were ordered to carry out the execution were used to bullying their prisoners.

"So, we hear your crime is to try to make yourself king of the Jews," they said. "See, Pilate's given us a notice to pin above you: 'Jesus of Nazareth – king of the Jews'. We'd better give you a crown then."

They twisted sharp thorns into a circle and rammed it onto Jesus' head. They hung a purple robe around his shoulders and began to mock.

"Long live the king!" they laughed. "Oh, sorry – we've got to kill you. A short reign, Your Majesty." Then they beat him to the ground and spat at him.

"Get up, you scum," they sneered. "Time to carry your cross to the place of execution."

The goaded him mercilessly through the streets of Jerusalem and beyond the city walls. There, on a hill, along with two criminals, they crucified him. Through the violence and pain, Jesus said a prayer.

"Forgive them, Father," said Jesus. "They don't know what they are doing."

As the afternoon light slowly drained away, Jesus hung, dying. He saw his disciple John standing next to his mother, and asked him to take care of her, as a dutiful son should. As he grew weaker, his head slumped. "Father, in your hands I place my spirit," he said. With that, he died. ✳

All those who knew Jesus, including the women who had followed him from Galilee, stood at a distance to watch.

Luke 23:49

JESUS IS RISEN

LUKE 23–24; JOHN 19–21

✳

WHEN JESUS DIED, IT SEEMED TO HIS FOLLOWERS THAT THE
GREAT MOVEMENT THEY HAD JOINED WAS OVER. THEN CAME
SOME ASTONISHING NEWS.

Not everyone at Jesus' trial had wanted his
death. Joseph, from the town of Arimathea,
was a good and honourable man. He was eager
to see God's kingdom come about, and he had
respected Jesus' teaching on this matter. After
the crucifixion, he went to Pilate and asked for
permission to take Jesus' body. He and his helpers
wrapped it for burial and took it to a rock-cut
tomb. By now, the sun was setting and the sabbath
day of rest was about to begin. Hurriedly they
rolled the stone door shut and went away.

The day of rest came and went. Early on the
Sunday morning, while it was still dark, one of
Jesus' most devoted followers went to the tomb:
Mary Magdalene. To her dismay, she found that
the door had been rolled open.

Weeping with grief and fear, she ran to tell
Simon Peter and John.

"Someone has taken the body away," she cried.
"I don't know where they have put him."

The two men ran to see for themselves. They

found the cloths that had been used to wrap the body folded up. Stunned by the sight, they went back home, each trying to work out what could have happened.

Mary stood outside the tomb, weeping. When she bent down to look inside one more time, she saw two angels dressed in white sitting there.

"Why are you crying?" they asked her.

"They have taken the body of Jesus and I don't know where they have put him," she sobbed.

Then she turned and saw a man. "Why are you crying?" he said in a concerned voice. "Who are you looking for?"

Mary thought it must be the gardener. "Did you take him, sir?" she asked. "Tell me where you put the body, so I can go there."

The man simply said her name: "Mary."

Then she knew: it was Jesus.

"Don't cling on to me," he said. "Go and tell my followers that the time has come for me to return to my Father." ꙮ

Jesus said to Mary, "Tell my brothers that I am returning to him who is my Father and their Father, my God and their God."

JOHN 20:17

291

Jesus' disciples took little comfort from her extraordinary story. They were afraid that the religious leaders who had condemned Jesus would be looking for them. When evening came, ten of the loyal eleven huddled in a room together with the door firmly locked.

Suddenly, Jesus was there with them, greeting them in the customary way: "Peace be with you."

He held up his hands, which clearly showed the wounds of the crucifixion, and smiled. The disciples' disbelief turned to joy. Their master was alive! He was telling them how they must carry on the work he had begun.

Jesus had gone by the time the eleventh disciple returned.

"We have seen Jesus alive!" they told him.

Thomas was scornful. "Unless I touch Jesus' wounds, I'm not going to fall for your story," he sneered. "Though I can't think why you'd make up such a ridiculous tale in this awful situation."

A week passed. Once again, the disciples were together in a locked room, only this time Thomas was with them. Again Jesus came and greeted them.

He spoke directly to Thomas. "Look at my hands; touch my wounds. Stop your doubting and believe."

Thomas simply replied, "My Lord and my God."

There was one more memorable meeting with Jesus. It happened when seven of the disciples had

Jesus said to Thomas, "How happy are those who believe without seeing me!"

JOHN 20:29

returned to Galilee. There, Simon Peter announced
that he was going fishing – returning to the work
that he knew so well.

The others were happy to join him and help cast
the nets over the water all through the night. By
morning, however, they had not caught a single
fish. Then they saw a lone figure on the shore
waving at them.

"Throw your net out on the right," he shouted.
With a shrug, the men decided to give it a try.
Almost at once, they knew they had made a catch,
but now they could not haul the net back, as it
was so full. John gazed at the stranger and said to
Simon Peter, "It's Jesus." ✎

At that, Simon Peter jumped overboard and swam to shore, leaving the others to pull the net and the boat in. They found that Jesus had a charcoal fire burning and was cooking fish to go with some loaves of bread.

"Come and eat," he said. "There is plenty to share."

After they had eaten, Jesus went to talk to Simon Peter.

"So, do you love me more than the other disciples do?" he asked.

"Yes, you know I do," replied Simon Peter. He was remembering with shame how his bold boast of loyalty on the night Jesus was arrested was followed by denying three times that he knew Jesus.

A second time and a third Jesus asked, and Simon Peter gave the same reply.

"Then you must take care of my flock of followers," Jesus told him. "Stop fretting about how much I value you, and whether or not you're more important to me than John is.

"You face a hard future. In the end, you will lose the freedom you have enjoyed up until now. There is just one thing to remember: follow me." ✳

Jesus said to Simon Peter, "Follow me!"

JOHN 21:19

PENTECOST

ACTS 1–5

✳

WHEN JESUS RETURNED TO HEAVEN, IT WAS TIME FOR HIS
FOLLOWERS TO CONTINUE THE WORK HE HAD BEGUN. THEY
RECEIVED STRENGTH FROM GOD: THE HOLY SPIRIT.

*Jesus told his
disciples, "You
will be witnesses
for me... to
the ends of the
earth."*

ACTS 1:8

For forty days after his death, Jesus appeared to
his followers many times. He talked with them
about the kingdom of God, and they were eager to
know if it would soon be established.

"It is not for me to say when the kingdom
will come," Jesus told them. "Only my Father
God knows that. However, I know that God will
strengthen you with the Holy Spirit. When that
happens, you are to go and spread the news about
me all over the world."

As Jesus finished saying this, a cloud settled
around him. When it melted into the sky, Jesus
was gone.

The disciples stood there, looking upwards. Two
angels dressed in white came and stood beside
them.

"Don't just stand there looking at the sky," they
said. "Jesus has gone up to heaven. One day, he
will return in the same way." ✌

It was time to move on. The disciples agreed that it was right to find someone to take the place of Judas Iscariot. (Following his betrayal of Jesus, he had hanged himself in shame.) After much prayer, they chose Matthias. Now there were twelve apostles – men who were willing to fulfil Jesus' instructions and spread the news of the kingdom.

Not long after came the harvest festival called Pentecost. All the believers were in a room together in Jerusalem. Suddenly, they heard a noise like a rushing wind. A dazzling brightness, like dancing flames, swept over them. They felt the power of God's Holy Spirit making them strong and bold. They began to speak in languages they had not learned, and they spilled out into the street, laughing and dancing.

The streets of Jerusalem were crowded. Pilgrims had come from many different places for the festival. They were astonished to hear these locals speaking in their own languages. Others laughed at how the believers were behaving. "They're just drunk," they jeered.

Peter stood up and began to address the crowd.

"Fellow Jews, and all who live in Jerusalem, listen while I explain.

"We are not drunk – it is only nine o'clock in the morning, after all. ✍

299

"Today, a prophecy is coming true. God is pouring out his Holy Spirit on those who turn to him. All this is because of Jesus."

He went on to explain what he now believed more firmly than ever. Jesus, whom people had seen crucified, was alive. God had shown that he was truly the messiah, the Christ.

"This is what you must do," declared Peter. "Turn away from the things that are not pleasing to God. Be baptized in the name of Jesus Christ. Then your sins will be forgiven, and you too will be strengthened by God's Holy Spirit."

The words were convincing. That day alone, three thousand people joined the group of believers. They began meeting together whenever they could: talking, listening, sharing meals, and praying. They began to share their possessions, so that no one was left in need. Day after day, they went as one group to the Temple. Then something astonishing happened. A man who could not walk sat at one of the Temple gates, begging. One day, he asked Peter and John for money.

"We have none to give," Peter had replied. "Even so,

I will give you what I can in the name of Jesus
Christ of Nazareth."

With that, he pulled the man to his feet. All
at once he began walking and jumping and
shouting loud thanks to God. Peter seized another
opportunity to preach to the astonished crowd.

Meanwhile, the chief priests and religious leaders
grew more and more concerned. They summoned
Peter and John and ordered them to stop leading
people astray with their strange beliefs about
Jesus. When they found out that the men had
not obeyed, they had them arrested and thrown
into prison. In a turn of events that the apostles
claimed was a miracle, the gates were unlocked and
the men walked free.

The religious leaders hurried to have them
rearrested. They held an urgent meeting to decide
what to do next. Then one of their number,
Gamaliel, came up with a wise approach.

"We should leave these men alone," he said. "If
their preaching is nonsense of their own invention,
it will come to nothing. If, however, there is truth
in what they say, we could find ourselves fighting
against God."

With that, the apostles were set free. They
spent every day at the Temple or in the homes of
believers, teaching and preaching about Jesus. ✷

A MARTYR AND A CONVERT

ACTS 6–9

✳

ONE OF THE GREATEST ENEMIES OF THE FOLLOWERS OF
JESUS WAS SAUL. HOWEVER, HE WAS TO BECOME THEIR MOST
DETERMINED CHAMPION.

The number of believers in Jerusalem kept on
growing. The daily life of the young church
became more and more complicated. Soon there
were arguments about whether or not everybody
was receiving their fair share of the group's funds.
As the apostles wanted to give all their attention
to preaching, they chose seven people to be in
charge of practical matters.

One of these helpers was a young man named
Stephen. He had a very good understanding of his
new faith and was able to put it clearly and simply.

His clever speaking was not well liked by
everyone. There were some Jews who hated not
being able to dismiss what he said with their
own arguments. They grew so angry that they
bribed some people to say that Stephen had been
disrespectful about God and Moses. The religious
leaders seized their chance to put the young
believer on trial.

Stephen was not in the least daunted. When it
was his turn to state his case, he recalled stories

from the Scriptures. He used them to show that, time and again, the Jewish people had failed to see what God was doing for them. "Now you are doing the same," he told his listeners. "God sent his servant into the world, as he promised long ago. You betrayed and murdered him. You say you are the guardians of the Law, but you have not obeyed it."

In the courtroom, the religious leaders began to murmur angrily. Stephen went on.

"Even now," he said, "I can see heaven opened and Jesus at God's right hand."

There was a howl of rage as everyone in the room rushed at Stephen with unseemly fury. He was hustled into the street and then out of the city. A lynch mob gathered, their eyes steely with hatred. They took off their coats and left them in the charge of a self-righteous young scholar named Saul. With brutal determination, Stephen's enemies hurled stones at the young believer until he was dead. ✌

Before he died, Stephen said, "Lord! Do not remember this sin against them!"

ACTS 7:60

From the day Stephen was martyred, the religious leaders began to persecute the church in Jerusalem severely. The believers were forced to go elsewhere, and wherever they went, they preached about Jesus and made more converts.

Saul did all he could to destroy the church. He went from house to house to find believers and had them flung into jail. When he realized that his efforts in Jerusalem were not going to be enough to stop the stories of Jesus spreading, he went to the high priest with a new request.

"Please will you write letters to the leaders of the synagogues in Damascus," he said. "If you explain my purpose to them, they will allow me to track down believers in that town. These so-called 'Followers of the Way of the Lord' are a menace to our faith."

The letters were prepared, and Saul started out with a band of travellers on the long journey north. They were getting near to Damascus when Saul saw a light flashing around him. Its brightness made him fall to the ground, and as he lay there, he heard a voice saying these words: "Saul, Saul, why do you persecute me?"

Saul was bewildered and afraid.

"Who are you?" he said sharply.

"I am Jesus, whom you persecute," came the reply. "Now get up and go to Damascus. There you will be told what to do next."

The other travellers had
watched Saul fall, and now they
saw him easing himself upright.
They had not seen anything unusual,
but they had heard a voice.

"I can't see," mumbled Saul.
"Something's happened to my eyes."

He stumbled forward and spoke in a
trembling voice. "I've gone blind," he
said. "Can someone take my hand and help
me?"

Slowly they all made their way to Damascus and
found a place for Saul to stay. He had no idea what
he was going to do and refused to eat or drink.

Meanwhile, there was a Christian in Damascus
named Ananias. As he was praying, he heard God
speaking to him. ✍

"Go to Straight Street," said the voice. "Ask for a man named Saul, whose hometown is Tarsus. He too is praying, and I have told him to expect someone named Ananias to come and cure his blindness."

Ananias was dismayed. "I've heard of Saul," he said. "I know his plans. He has come here to arrest everyone who believes in Jesus."

"Please do as I say," God replied. "I have chosen this Saul to tell everyone about me – Jews and Gentiles, kings and slaves."

Ananias obeyed. He not only cured Saul's blindness; he also baptized him as a new believer. When Saul recovered his strength, he began preaching in the synagogues. He told everyone that Jesus was the Son of God.

His preaching soon made him enemies. Some of the Jews in Damascus, who had been counting on his help, made plans to kill him. The believers found out that they were watching the city gates to see when he left the city. One night, his new friends took him to a lonely part of the city walls. There they let him down in a basket.

Saul went first to Jerusalem, but he soon found enemies there. The believers agreed that he should be sent back to his hometown of Tarsus. For the next few years, the Christians were left alone and the message about Jesus spread. ✳

New believers

✳

SAUL BECAME AN APOSTLE ALONGSIDE THOSE WHO HAD BEEN
JESUS' DISCIPLES. THEY, AND MANY OTHERS, CARRIED OUT JESUS'
INSTRUCTIONS TO SPREAD THEIR FAITH TO THE WORLD.

Peter was keen to travel widely, telling the news
about Jesus. On one occasion, he set off for
the towns on the coast.

In Joppa lived a woman named Tabitha. She was
much loved in her community, for she was good
and generous and spent long hours making clothes
to give to the poor.

One day, she became unwell and died.
The believers in Joppa heard that Peter
was nearby and asked him to come and
help. He arrived to find many of
Tabitha's friends gathered around
her body, weeping. When they left
the room, he knelt down and
prayed, "Tabitha, get up." At
once, she opened her eyes.

The news of the miracle
quickly spread, and as a result,
many people in the town
joined the number of
believers.

Peter was invited to stay in the town. One day, around noon, he went up onto the flat roof to pray. While he was there, he began to feel hungry. As if in a dream, he saw a sheet being lowered by its four corners from heaven. In it were all kinds of creatures. Peter heard a voice telling him to kill something to eat.

"I can't do that," replied Peter. "I've always kept the Jewish food laws strictly. I'm not going to break them and eat something unclean just for a moment's hunger."

"Don't call unclean the things that God says are clean," came the voice.

While Peter was puzzling over this, messengers came to the door calling for him. He went to find out what was going on.

"Our master, a Roman captain, Cornelius, has sent us here from Caesarea," said the men. "He takes a great interest in the Jewish faith and our synagogue. He believes God is telling him to invite you to his house."

Then Peter understood. Cornelius was a Gentile, and in the past Peter had thought it unclean to visit a Gentile home. Now it was the right thing to do. He went, and as a result of his preaching, Cornelius and all his household were baptized.

Peter told Cornelius, "Those who worship God and do what is right are acceptable to him, no matter what race they belong to."

ACTS 10:35

Meanwhile, a lively church had been established in Antioch, many miles further north. When it began, it had only Jewish members. However, it had grown to include Gentile believers as well. A man called Barnabas went to Antioch from Jerusalem to help with the preaching; he then went to Tarsus to look for Saul and invite him to join the church. The pair became highly respected and, not long after, undertook a special mission: to preach the news about Jesus in other parts of the Roman empire.

They went first to the island of Cyprus and then to the mainland of Asia, further north. Saul became better known by the Roman version of his name – Paul – as he and Barnabas went from place to place, preaching to both Jews and Gentiles. They had great success in convincing people to follow Jesus Christ. When at last they returned to Antioch, the church was delighted.

However, many Jewish believers were concerned at the number of Gentiles who now called themselves Christians. Paul and Barnabas were sent to a meeting with the apostles in Jerusalem to discuss the matter. There it was agreed that God himself had clearly blessed both Jews and Gentiles and that they should learn to live together while respecting each other's tradition.

Paul and Barnabas were eager to undertake more missions, but made separate plans. With new

"There is no difference between Jews and Gentiles, between slaves and free people, between men and women; you are all one in union with Christ Jesus."

PAUL'S LETTER TO THE GALATIANS, 3:28

companions, Paul went and preached across Asia
before sailing to the prosperous town of Philippi
in Macedonia. On the sabbath, they walked along
the riverside to the place where they had heard
some Jews would be meeting to pray. They came
across a group of Jewish women, who were pleased
to listen to what Paul had to say. One of them was
a wealthy woman named Lydia, who had made her
fortune in the luxury trade of purple cloth. She
asked that she and her household be baptized at
once.

"Come and stay in my house if you have decided
I am a true believer," she said. Paul and his
companions were delighted to accept her offer,
and continued to preach in the city. ❧

One day, as they were going to a place to pray, a young slave girl began screaming at them. She was in the grip of some malady that made her rant and rave, and for this her owners hired her out as a fortune teller. Paul, however, grew impatient when she cried out, "These men are servants of God! They can tell you how to be saved."

He spoke sharply. "In the name of Jesus Christ, leave that girl alone."

Whatever evil thing was within the girl left. The cure was good for the girl, but bad news for her owners: she no longer told fortunes. They had Paul and his friend Silas arrested and put on public trial immediately.

"These men are Jews and they are causing trouble in the city," they said. "They have no respect for our laws and customs."

A crowd soon gathered to hear the extravagant charges being made. They began chanting that they wanted the outsiders punished. The authorities had Paul and Silas whipped and thrown into jail.

Paul had already grown used to facing opposition. He and Silas went on praying and singing cheerful hymns well into the dark hours.

Around midnight, there was an earthquake. It shook open not only the prison doors but also the chains that bound the prisoners. The jailer himself was shaken out of slumber. When he saw the prison was open and that he faced punishment for neglecting his duties, he drew his sword to kill himself.

"Stop!" cried Paul. "We're all here."

Paul not only calmed the man down; he took his chance to preach to him about Jesus. The jailer asked to be baptized at once.

In the morning, the authorities sent officers with a message for Paul and Silas to be released.

"It's not as simple as you think," said Paul. "We were not found guilty of a crime, yet we were whipped and imprisoned. We are Roman citizens, and we don't deserve such abuse."

The authorities were dismayed to discover that they had mistreated Roman citizens. They hurried around, full of apologies, and begged them to leave the city quietly.

After saying goodbye to Lydia and other believers, they went on with the great mission. ✳

Paul wrote to the Philippians, "Don't worry about anything, but in all your prayers ask God for what you need, always asking him with a thankful heart."

PHILIPPIANS 4:6

To the End

Acts 19–28; 1 Corinthians 11–13

✳

The Bible ends with glimpses of churches in many parts of the Roman empire. In spite of the difficulties they faced, believers were confident that God would establish an everlasting kingdom.

Paul and the other apostles worked bravely to preach the news about Jesus as widely as they could. They faced many difficulties. Sometimes the Jews in local synagogues opposed their preaching, saying that they were being disrespectful to the Law and the Scriptures. Other times, the Gentile population branded them as troublemakers.

At Ephesus, for example, the townspeople made a lot of money from pilgrims who came to the temple of the goddess Diana. Paul preached that only God was worthy of worship. He said that other gods were not gods at all. The silversmiths who made souvenir models of Diana were enraged.

"If that fanatic gets a following, people will stop believing in Diana and the pilgrim trade will end," said one of the silversmiths. "Our livelihood will go with it. We must act decisively to stop him."

His speech sparked a riot. Two of Paul's companions were hustled to the town's open-air theatre, where the mood of the mob grew very ugly. Even though the town clerk managed to calm things down, it was agreed that Paul should travel on.

After several years of travelling and preaching, Paul announced that he wanted to return to Jerusalem. His friends warned him that he would not be safe there: many people in the city were suspicious of the believers and of Paul's role in preaching about Jesus.

They were right to be afraid: in Jerusalem, some of Paul's enemies brought trumped-up charges that he had taken Gentiles into the part of the Temple reserved for Jews. If this had been true, it would have been a serious crime.

Paul was put on trial. When he gave his defence, he used the opportunity to preach about Jesus. This only made his enemies angrier than before, and they hatched a plot to kill him.

It became clear that Paul would not get a fair trial in Jerusalem. He was sent to another court in Caesarea. There he asked to stand trial in the emperor's court in Rome, as was his right as a Roman citizen. ❧

Paul wrote to the Christians in Ephesus, "Pray on every occasion, as the Spirit leads."
EPHESIANS 6:18

His request was finally granted. Paul and some other prisoners were put on a grain ship bound for Italy and Rome. It was late in the season, however, and sea conditions were treacherous. The ship was caught in a violent storm that lasted for days.

"Don't be afraid," Paul told the sailors. "I am sure that God wants me to get to my trial. I believe we will survive this."

Even so, the storm did not let up. The sailors threw the cargo overboard to lighten the ship and tried to steer it on, desperately looking for land. Then one morning they noticed a bay with a beach and decided to try to run the ship onto it.

It was a bold and desperate plan… and it might have worked, but for the fact that the ship hit a sandbank in the shallower water and stuck fast a little way from shore.

"Everyone who can swim should jump now and head for the beach," ordered the officer in charge. "Those that can't swim – we'll give you a plank as a float and you must do the best you can."

The salt waves raced to the shore, and somehow everyone made it to the beach. They emerged from the water, shivering and spluttering. ❧

Everyone was made welcome at the place they had landed, on the island of Malta. There they spent the stormy winter months. In the spring, they set sail again and at long last Paul reached Rome.

Paul was made welcome by the Christians in the city. He was allowed to live under house arrest with a soldier guarding him while he waited for his trial. There he continued the work he had begun while he was on his travels: he wrote long letters to the young churches, many of which he had set up. He wanted the believers to understand their faith more deeply and to live in peace with one another, even though they came from many different backgrounds.

"When you meet," he reminded them, "remember this important ceremony. The Lord Jesus, on the night he was betrayed, took a piece of bread, gave thanks to God, broke it, and said, 'This is my body, which is for you. Do this in memory of me.' In the same way, after the supper, he took the cup and said, 'This cup is God's new covenant, sealed with my blood. Whenever you drink it, do so in memory of me.'

"Remember that you are now Christ's body on earth. Like a body, you are made up of different parts. Each has its own purpose, but each is vital to the whole.

"Whatever gifts and talents you have are nothing without love.

Paul wrote to the Christians in Corinth, "Every time you eat this bread and drink from this cup you proclaim the Lord's death until he comes."

I CORINTHIANS 11:26

"Love is patient and kind; it is not jealous or conceited or proud; love is not ill-mannered or selfish or irritable; love does not keep a record of wrongs; love is not happy with evil, but is happy with the truth. Love never gives up; and its faith, hope, and patience never fail."

These words of Paul and the words of other apostles inspired Christians everywhere to keep the faith. Those that did were able to face the many troubles that came their way. They believed that, as Jesus had been raised from the tomb, death would not be the end. They trusted that Jesus would one day return, and they would be safe in God's love for ever. ✳

"Meanwhile these three remain: faith, hope, and love; and the greatest of these is love."

I CORINTHIANS 13:13